"In this clear, accessible, informative, ... or the *For Beginners* series, Toni Morrison, America's only living Nobel Laureate in Literature, comes to life. The collection is dense with information and detail. The reader learns not only the facts about one of the world's most contemporary authors, but the nuances and details regarding her biographical context—personal and familial relationship, race relations, feminism, class complexities, literary and cultural influences, historical intersections and much more. The narrative intersperses the biographical with a brief plot summary of each of Morrison's works that include commentary on what inspired the author to embark on the work and the critical reception each work received. Each of these discussions is designed to encourage the reader to read and explore Morrison's work. One of the most compelling sections of the work is the reader's companion contained in the section called "Her Work: Reinventing the Novel." This helpful guide provides literary critical information about Morrison's work in an accessible and encouraging format, which can only enrich the reader's encounter with Morrison's writings. Although, at times, the critical guide oversteps the boundary between opinion and analysis, generally the information presented aims to encourage careful and informed interaction with Morrison's works. The same can be said of the close readings of each of Morrison's texts. Particularly useful in those sections are the background notes that define and explain terms of literary analysis or historical context. This volume is highly recommended both for novice Morrison readers and for anyone in need of a rich, yet straightforward synopsis and analysis of the canon of one of the world's most important contemporary writers."

—Carmen Gillespie
Professor of English, Bucknell University; Director, Griot Institute of
Africana Studies; and author, *A Critical Companion to Toni Morrison*
(2008) and *Toni Morrison: Forty Years in the Clearing* (2012)

TONI MORRISON
FOR BEGINNERS ®

BY
RON DAVID

ILLUSTRATIONS BY
DIRK SHEARER

FOREWORD BY
ELIZABETH BEAULIEU

FOR BEGINNERS®

For Beginners LLC
155 Main Street, Suite 211
Danbury, CT 06810 USA
www.forbeginnersbooks.com

Cataloging-in-Publication information is available from the
Library of Congress.

ISBN # 978-1-939994-54-7 Trade

Manufactured in the United States of America

For Beginners® and Beginners Documentary Comic Books®
are published by For Beginners LLC.

First Edition

10 9 8 7 6 5 4 3 2 1

CONTENTS

FOREWORD

by Elizabeth Beaulieu

Toni Morrison's works offer many gifts to the careful reader: prose that both sings and paints, themes that universalize the African American condition, inspiration to continue believing that the human soul will triumph over adversity, a mother's touch, an elder's wisdom. But Morrison's works also challenge the reader; she crafts stories that are vexing in content and form. Why would a little black girl want blue eyes? Can a Milkman fly, and if he could, why would he? Is killing one's child ever the moral choice? What and where is home? And why, many an exasperated reader has asked, doesn't she tell a tale directly?

"Life is large," Morrison is fond of saying when she is accused of crafting stories that are larger than life. She wants her readers to be open to every possibility, to consider questions and situations they may never encounter on their own, to enter into the gaps she intentionally leaves in her narratives. This allows Morrison and her reader to co-create a story that is at once powerful and personal.

One of the best ways to approach Morrison's work is to think of it as an invitation to inquiry; any reader, whether beginner or advanced, can find a way in by answering the question, "What am I curious about?" The avenue in might be, for example, word play, music, popular culture, history, racial or gender identity, motherhood, folklore, myth. The realities her novels engage are often difficult—family dynamics, the politics of race, oppression, incest, infanticide. But these realities are human realities, and Morrison explores and exploits them in a uniquely American context. She enlivens previously silenced voices and honors their struggles. The engaged reader, by accepting Morrison's invitation to inquire and to participate in the storytelling, is drawn into the struggle and ultimately called to act with courage at the conclusion of the reading experience.

From writing-group member to Nobel laureate and beyond,

Morrison has written while mothering, while teaching, while working as an editor, while living as a Black woman in still-racist America. She has inspired all sorts of readers by crafting the stories that she didn't get to read as a young person and by doing so in a way that resonates across race, gender, and social class. She has secured a place in the canon alongside William Faulkner and Virginia Woolf, the two writers about whom she wrote her master's thesis, and she is continuing to write well into her eighties, publishing most recently *God Help the Child* (2015). In an interview with *Guardian* reporter Emma Brockes, Morrison said, "I feel totally curious and alive and in control. And almost ... magnificent, when I write" (April 13, 2014).

In her 1993 Nobel address, Morrison tells the story of the blind old wise woman who is asked by several impudent youngsters whether the bird they are holding is dead or alive. Refusing to be taunted, the wise woman replies, "I don't know ... I don't know whether the bird you are holding is dead or alive, but what I do know is that it is in your hands. It is in your hands." Morrison goes on to tell us that the bird is language, and that each of us holds language, with its infinite potential, in our hands. Is it dead or alive? It is up to us.

You are holding in your hands now a book that will help you understand and value this wise woman's work. It is in your hands to accept the invitation; her gifts beckon. In perhaps the most quoted lines of her Nobel address, Morrison says, "Word-work is sublime ... because it is generative; it makes meaning that secures our difference, our human difference—the way in which we are like no other life. We die. That may be the meaning of life. But we do language. That may be the measure of our lives." You, too, can be magnificent by joining in Morrison's word-work.

> *Dr. Elizabeth Beaulieu* is associate professor and dean of the Core Division at Champlain College in Burlington, Vermont. She is the editor of *The Toni Morrison Encyclopedia* (2003) and of *Writing African American Women: An Encyclopedia of Literature by and about Women of Color* (2006), as well as the author of *Black Women Writers and the American Neo-Slave Narrative: Femininity Unfettered* (1999).

INTRODUCTION

After her divorce in 1964, Toni Morrison found herself in a situation that women everywhere can relate to: she had no husband, she had one child and another on the way, and she was jobless with no prospects for employment. So at the age of 33, Morrison returned to her parents' home in Ohio.

For Toni Morrison, it was the beginning of an astonishing rebirth.

Twenty-nine years and six novels later, she won the Nobel Prize in Literature. That meant, among other things, that her face would grace a Swedish postage stamp, that she'd get $825,000 in spare change, and that, as of 1993, she was considered the best writer in the world. Not the best *woman* writer. Not the best *black* writer. The best writer, *period*!

So if you haven't read Toni Morrison, this book will introduce you to her novels—plot descriptions, subtexts, reviews, and Morrison's comments on her work. On the other hand, if you *have* read—or attempted to read—Toni Morrison, you may need this book even more.

Many people consider Morrison's novels difficult to read. Most of her readers have at least one book on their shelves that they couldn't finish or, when they did finish one, just scratched their heads in confusion. Although Morrison sells truckloads of books and is among the best-known writers in the world, much of the time, if we're honest about it, we aren't entirely sure what this literary Conjure Woman is talking about. And when we are sure, it turns out we were half-wrong or only got the tip of the iceberg instead of the whole, beautiful, brooding thing.

So here is the book you need to get friendly with Toni Morrison. It's about the woman, her books, her mission, her wordmusic, and all that writing she does between the lines ... what writers call "the subtext." Morrison's books are like the ocean: the surface is beautiful but everything that gives them life lies beneath.

She's the kind of writer who can change your life.

With most writers, you can examine their books and leave it at that. With Morrison, her life is as extraordinary as her books. She didn't even start writing until she was 35, all the while holding down a full-time job and raising two children. Her first novel wasn't published until she was nearly 40, yet she managed to become the first black woman to win the Nobel Prize in Literature. Not only did she blossom into what critic John Leonard called "the best writer working in America today," but she also became one of the most impactful editors in the world.

The enormity of her talent raises a question that begs for an answer: As a writer, Toni Morrison is one of the most magical beings ever to grow out of the earth—but as a human being, she is so, so, normal, that you wonder how somebody that normal can have the power to move us so much?

Before you're finished asking it, the question answers itself: Morrison's power to move us, to involve us, is grounded in her very normalness, her so-much-like-us-ness. She has lived through the soul-shriveling experiences of an "ordinary" life, including divorce, depression, racism, single motherhood, and being broke and friendless in a strange town.

So who is this woman?

To see Toni Morrison as she sees herself, you have to look beyond her own life.

For Morrison, life begins with the lives of her ancestors—

...with West African *griots* telling magical stories to people who listen with their bodies and respond with their lives.

...with the millions of men, women, and children killed in Africa or during the Middle Passage, to whom she dedicated her shattering novel *Beloved*.

...with the 15 million Africans who were "lucky" enough to make it all the way to America, only to be enslaved.

...with her grandmother, who left her home in the South with seven children and $30 because she feared white sexual violence against her daughters.

...with her aunts, great-aunts, uncles—all of these and more—they are all her ancestors.

People today tend to talk about their ancestors as if they were an abstraction, a "concept." Toni Morrison's ancestors aren't a concept—they are *real*. And sooner or later, as she told Judith Wilson of *Essence* magazine, she was going to have to face them:

> **Since it was possible for my mother, my grandmother and her mother to do what they did ... snatching children and running away from the South and living in a big city trying to stay alive when you can't even read the road signs ... I know I can't go to those women and say, "Well, you know, my life is so hard." They don't want to hear that! I don't want to meet them people nowhere—ever!—and have them look at me and say, "What were you doing back there?"**

Got your head around that? Good. Now we can move on to the normal stuff.

If you study the culture and art of African-Americans, you are not studying a regional or minor culture. What you are studying is America.

—Toni Morrison to Charlie Rose

HER LIFE

Chloe Anthony Wofford

Toni Morrison was born Chloe Anthony Wofford—on February 18, 1931—in the steel-mill town of Lorain, Ohio. Her father, George, was a shipyard welder from Georgia. Her mother, Ramah Willis Wofford, came from Alabama. Morrison's maternal grandfather, John Solomon Willis, was an ex-slave who had owned 88 acres of land in Alabama until some white Southern gentlemen cheated him out of it. Mr. Willis decided he'd had enough of the South and worked his family north to Lorain, a small industrial town west of Cleveland on Lake Erie. Lorain was full of European immigrants and Southern blacks who'd come to work in the steel mills.

Chloe's father George was a hard-working man who held down three jobs at the same time during the Great Depression. He grew up in Georgia amidst the lynching of young black men. He told his children that there would never be harmony between the races because white people didn't have the brains to overcome the bigotry they were taught as children.

Chloe's mother Ramah (a name picked at random from the Bible) felt that people who grew up in a racist society could eventually be changed by education. (But she wasn't going to hold her breath until it happened!)

Chloe, the second of four children, was quiet, kept to herself, and liked books. In her teens she read the masterpieces of European literature. She loved Dostoevsky, Tolstoy, and especially the English writer Jane Austen. "Those books were not written for a little black girl in Lorain, Ohio," she told *Newsweek* magazine in 1981, "but they were so magnificently done that I got them anyway."

Chloe never thought of being a writer, but without realizing it, she absorbed the folktales and songs that were part of Southern black culture. One children's song her mother's family sang began with the words, "Green, the only son of Solomon." It was a song Morrison would use as the turning point in one of her most famous novels.

At age 17, Chloe left Ohio to attend Howard University in Washington, D.C.

Howard University

Founded in 1867 by white clergymen, Howard started as a school for black preachers and evolved into one of the best colleges in the country. It was home to legendary educators like Alain Locke, the philosopher/poet who spearheaded the Harlem Renaissance in the 1920s, and Sterling A. Brown, the poet/professor who helped establish African American literary criticism. Among the university's graduates were former Supreme Court Justice Thurgood Marshall, opera singer Jessye Norman, and actor Ossie Davis.

Chloe chose to major in English even though black literary consciousness was still in its infancy in the 1940s. Even at a black college like Howard, great writers like Langston Hughes and Zora Neale Hurston were not widely read. Chloe, who wanted to be a dancer, changed her name to Toni and joined the Howard University Players' tours of the Deep South. Seeing what life was like for Southern blacks gave her a taste of the racism her parents had endured.

After graduation, Toni attended Cornell University for her master's degree in English. Her thesis—foreshadowing the style of her writing and her predilection for grim subject matter—was on the theme of suicide in the novels of William Faulkner and Virginia Woolf. After Cornell, Toni taught English at Texas Southern University in Houston, where she began to think of black culture as a subject for formal study. "Before that it had only been on a very personal level—my family," she would say.

Toni returned to Howard University in 1957 as an English teacher and met people who would play key roles in the struggle

for African American equality: the radical poet Amiri Baraka (then LeRoi Jones); Andrew Young, future mayor of Atlanta and U.S. ambassador to the United Nations; and Stokely Carmichael (later Kwame Touré), a lively wisecracker who stood in the front lines of the Civil Rights and Black Power movements of the 1960s.

Marriage

While teaching at Howard, Toni fell in love with a young architect from Jamaica named Harold Morrison. They were married in 1958. Their first son, Harold Ford, was born in 1961. Although she continued to teach, Toni began to feel restless. She joined a writers' group, not because she wanted to write but because she wanted the company of interesting people.

Each member of the group had to bring in a story. One week, Toni ran out of old writings to bring and, knowing that she had to dash off something new, remembered a conversation she'd had with another little black girl growing up in Ohio. The girl said she had stopped believing in God because, after two years of praying for blue eyes, God still hadn't given them to her. Morrison quickly wrote the story, read it to the writers' group, and put it in a drawer.

In 1964, pregnant with her second child, Morrison quit her job at Howard and took a trip to Europe with her husband and son. By the time she returned, the marriage had ended. In later years she would look back on this as a time of emptiness and confusion: "It was as though I had nothing left but my imagination. I had no will, no judgment, no perspective, no power, no authority, no self—just this brutal sense of irony, melancholy and a trembling respect for words."

Toni Morrison found herself in a position that women everywhere can relate to: no husband, one child and another on the way, and jobless with no prospects for employment.

At the age of 33, depressed and confused, she returned to her parents' home in Lorain.

The Syracuse Blues

Not long after the birth of her second son, Slade Kevin, Morrison left Ohio to take a job as a textbook editor in Syracuse, New York. Mornings, she would leave little Harold and Slade with the housekeeper while she went to work. After work, like working mothers everywhere, she would make dinner for her sons and spend a few hours with them until their bedtime.

Although she lived in Syracuse for two full years, Morrison made no friends. Working from nine to five, caring for her sons, and having no social life, Morrison grew increasingly depressed. One night, in the quiet hours when her sons slept, she picked up a notebook and began to write. As the words washed through her, she began to feel that writing might be a way to escape the desperation she felt in this cold, lonely city. As she wrote, the characters she wrote about began taking on lives of their own ... and making demands of their own. They wanted or seemed to want (she wondered if she was going crazy for thinking words on a piece of paper could *want* anything) the little scrap of story she'd written years ago. So, during the Syracuse winter of 1967, Toni Morrison dug up the story about the little girl who prayed for blue eyes...

What was going on in Morrison's head? Why does a 35-year-old woman suddenly begin writing a novel? Indeed it took years before Morrison understood her own journey. More than ten years later, in a 1978 interview with Jane Bakerman for *Black American Literature Forum*, she still sounded mystified:

> *I was in a place where there was nobody I could talk to and have real conversations with. I was also very unhappy. So I wrote then, for that reason.*

In 1983, some 15 years after the fact, she told literary critic Claudia Tate:

> *It happened after my father died. It happened after my divorce. It has happened other times. Now I know how to bring it about without going through the actual event. It's exactly what Guitar [a character in Song of Solomon] said: "when you release all the shit, then you can fly."*

After working all day as an editor, Morrison would return home each night to her writing. Whether it was published or not, she knew she couldn't stop writing this, this ... novel. She called it *The Bluest Eye*. Sometimes she would think, "No one is ever going to read this until I'm dead."

The Bluest Eye
The Bluest Eye is the story of three black schoolgirls growing up in Ohio, the sisters Claudia and Frieda McTeer and their friend Pecola Breedlove. Claudia, who tells much of the story, is a strong-willed eight-year-old. Pecola, her 11-year-old friend, thinks her life would be perfect if only she could have blue eyes.

Afterword: New York City

After several rejections, *The Bluest Eye* was published in 1970. By that time, TM was living in New York City and working as an editor for Random House. She had worked her way into the trade division, where she could edit books by prominent black Americans (Muhammad Ali, Andrew Young, and Angela Davis, among others) and help develop the careers of promising black women writers (such as Toni Cade Bambara and Gayl Jones). "Toni has done more to encourage and publish other black writers than anyone I know," Young told *Newsweek*.

The Bluest Eye was not a commercial success, but it did fairly well with critics. Neither TM nor the critics realized that she would become one of the premier novelists of her time. But that barely mattered for Morrison, who had discovered her magic.

Through a Glass Darkly...

Even though her novel wasn't a great success, Morrison was suddenly considered an authority on black cultural issues. She was publishing articles and book reviews, but she began to worry. Months had passed since she finished *The Bluest Eye*, and she didn't have an idea for another book. Maybe that was it—maybe she'd never write another novel?

It was the early 1970s. The Women's Liberation movement was gaining ground, but it struck TM as hopelessly, myopically, white-middle-class. Her irritation with the movement sparked an idea. Apparently, these newly enlightened white ladies had decided that it was time for women to start loving one another, to begin being sisters and friends. But what did they mean *begin*, Morrison wondered? All her life, Toni had helped and been helped by her family and friends. Now she decided to try something that had rarely, if ever, been attempted in American fiction: to deeply explore a friendship between two black women.

Sula

The relationship between Nel Wright and Sula Peace is unique. Even as little girls, they are bound together by a terrible secret. Sula leaves town, returns years later, and betrays Nel, putting their friendship to the test.

Published in December 1973, *Sula* brought Toni Morrison national recognition. The novel was excerpted in *Redbook* magazine and nominated for the 1975 National Book Award. There was a bit of a controversy, however, when Sara Blackburn wrote in *The New York Times Book Review* that the novel lacked "the stinging immediacy" of Morrison's nonfiction.

The author's testy response: "She's talking about my life. It has a stinging immediacy for me."

The Black Book and *Song of Solomon*

Two months after the publication of *Sula*, Random House published *The Black Book*—described by Bill Cosby in the introduction as the kind of scrapbook we'd have "if a 300-year-old black man had decided to keep a record of what it was like for himself and his people." This anthology of 300 years of African American life was compiled by historian and collector Middleton "Spike" Harris, and edited—as well as inspired by—Toni Morrison.

Working on the collection, Morrison sat in Harris's apartment reading 200- and 300-year-old newspaper accounts of the tortures inflicted upon slaves. Among the newspaper clippings she found an 1856 article about a runaway slave who killed her own daughter rather than see her returned to slavery. Years later, this unthinkable episode would be the inspiration for Morrison's most acclaimed novel.

In the meantime, another novel was coming together in TM's mind. Because *Sula* had received so much attention for its strong female characters, naturally the fiercely unpredictable Morrison decided to write a novel powered by *men*.

But this was another difficult time in her personal life. She had money problems, her oldest son was entering manhood a bit too energetically, and her father died. TM went to Ohio for his funeral and couldn't stop thinking about him after returning to New York. As she worked on her new novel, she had long conversations with him in her head. She needed her father's help to write this difficult new book about men. The result was one of the most astonishing novels of the century.

Song of Solomon

Macon Dead III—everyone calls him Milkman—leaves his home in Michigan and travels to the South in search of the fabled family fortune, a hidden treasure of gold. Although he never finds the gold, Milkman finds something more important.

Song of Solomon is a sweeping epic, much larger than the story of Milkman's quest. Morrison's description of her own book: "It's about black people who could fly."

Aftersong

The publication of *Song of Solomon* (1977) changed Morrison's life. At the age of 46, she was an "overnight success." *Song* was the first novel by a black writer to be named a Book-of-the-Month Club selection since Richard Wright's *Native Son* in 1940. *Song of Solomon* became a paperback bestseller, TM received the National Book Critics Circle Award, and President Jimmy Carter appointed her to the National Council on the Arts.

Despite her success, Morrison continued to work full-time at Random House, teach at Yale every Friday, and be both father and mother to her sons. Not long after the publication of her third novel, TM dropped off her son

Harold at his Manhattan piano lesson and drove aimlessly around the city to kill time. As she passed a Doubleday bookstore, she noticed a large display of books in the window. It took her a few beats to recognize the cover of *Song of Solomon*—accompanied by a huge sign: "A Triumph, by Toni Morrison."

Literary Novelty, Media Event

Morrison, on the prowl for her next book, began reasoning, ruminating, and researching her way into another novel. It was so different from her other work, so audacious, so ... No reputable novelist would base a serious literary novel on an old African folktale that most people know as one of those silly old Uncle Remus stories ... would they? (*lickety split, lickety split*)

America generally does not make media stars of its authors. Norman Mailer never had his own line of 100-dollar Nike sneakers ("Air" Mailers?); nobody ever asked Joyce Carol Oates to host *Saturday Night Live*. But Toni Morrison was being peddled like a rock star. She wasn't "just" a writer, she was a celebrity. And *Tar Baby* wasn't just a book, it was a media event.

Tar Baby
Tar Baby, built on a foundation of black folklore and set on a Caribbean island, is a modern love story between Jadine, a beautiful, pampered black model, and an earthy dreadlocked outlaw named Son.

After the publication of *Tar Baby*, Morrison achieved the ultimate sign of success in America: "Are you really going to put a middle-aged, gray-haired colored lady on the cover of this magazine?" she asked. In March 1981, TM became the first black woman to appear on the cover of *Newsweek*. She was literature's biggest star since Hemingway. After the *Newsweek* cover, publications everywhere featured articles on her. People were dazzled by the range of her activities: raising two sons, full-time job as an editor, teaching college, writing four novels— they called her Superwoman! *Tar Baby* stayed on the bestseller list for four months even though most critics considered it a disappointment.

Dreaming Emmett

In 1983, after 20 years of midwifing some of the seminal moments of the African American literary revolution of the 1970s, TM left Random House. In 1984, she was named Albert Schweitzer Professor of the Humanities at the State University of New York in Albany.

It was in Albany that Toni Morrison began working on her first play.

Emmett Till was a black Chicago teenager who, while visiting his uncle in Mississippi in 1955, was accused of whistling at a white woman. Till, just 14, was shot in the head and thrown into a river. The white men charged with his murder were acquitted by an all-white jury. Because of its flagrant brutality and injustice, the Till murder became a rallying point for the early Civil Rights movement. In Morrison's stage play, titled *Dreaming Emmett*, Emmett Till was allowed to speak on his own behalf. He was brought back from the dead to describe his murder in his own words...

It Belonged to Life, Not Art

Morrison's next major work also had its origins in a violent historical incident—the story of the woman she'd read about while doing research for *The Black Book*. In 1856, a Kentucky slave named Margaret Garner escaped from her master's plantation and fled with her four children across the frozen Ohio River to Cincinnati.

When finally tracked down by slave-catchers, Garner tried to kill her children so they wouldn't be returned to the horrors of slavery. For years after reading about her, TM wanted to write Garner's story but couldn't. It wouldn't come out. Morrison decided the story simply couldn't be written. It belonged to life, not to art. Then she wrote it.

> ### *Beloved*
> **Sethe is struggling to create a new life for herself despite the fact that her house is haunted by the ghost of the baby she killed 18 years earlier. Paul D. (a former slave) tries to cast out the baby's spirit and seems to have succeeded until a beautiful 20-year-old stranger with a scar on her throat arrives at Sethe's house.**

Beloved (1987) was quickly acclaimed as Morrison's most powerful novel. John Leonard called it "a masterwork." Novelist Margaret Atwood wrote that Morrison's "versatility and technical and emotional range appear to know no bounds."

Despite its acclaim, *Beloved* failed to win either the National Book Award or the National Book Critics Circle Award. In January 1988, 49 black writers and critics published a signed tribute to Morrison's achievements in *The New York Times Book Review*, chastising the good old boys on the committees for not giving either award to Morrison.

On March 31, 1988, *Beloved* won the Pulitzer Prize. Said Morrison, "I am glad that the merits of the book were allowed to surface and be the only consideration of the Pulitzer Prize committee." To nobody's surprise, she began working on another novel…

Jazz … and BAM!!!

Years before she thought of writing *Beloved*, TM had seen a book by the photographer James Van Der Zee called *The Harlem Book of the Dead*, a collection of photographs of deceased black New Yorkers taken in the 1920s. One photo that intrigued Morrison was a picture of a dead girl lying in a coffin. The accompanying text explained that the 18-year-old girl had been dancing at a "rent party" when she was shot…

> ### Jazz
>
> Joe Trace, a middle-aged salesman, falls in love with 18 year-old Dorcas, "with one of those deepdown, spooky loves that he had to shoot her just to keep the feeling going." Joe's wife crashes the funeral and tries to disfigure the dead girl's face.

In contrast to the overwhelming critical acclaim for *Beloved*, the response to *Jazz* was disappointing. Despite the luke-warm reviews, everyone seemed to want an opinion from TM on everything. And she didn't disappoint, sharing her views on everything from the Rodney King riots to teen pregnancy. Then, BAM!!!

ON OCTOBER 7, 1993, THE NOBEL COMMITTEE OF THE SWEDISH ACADEMY ANNOUNCED THAT TONI MORRISON HAD WON THE NOBEL PRIZE IN LITERATURE.

Morrison's acceptance speech to the Swedish Academy—on language, its debasement, and the responsibility of those who use it—was stirring. "For the first time in the memory of the Foreign Ministry," John

Leonard reported, "the audience, unable to help itself, stood for a second standing ovation."

She was the first black woman to win the Nobel Prize in Literature.

Aftermath: Fire and *Paradise*

Two weeks after she won the Nobel Prize, Morrison's house caught fire and burned to the ground. She went to work on a new novel.

The book was inspired by an obscure bit of American history. After the Civil War, former slaves traveled to sparsely populated Western states—the ones we usually identify with cowboys—to set up all-black towns. The settlers placed ads in newspapers seeming to invite black people to join their new communities ... with the enigmatic warning, "Come Prepared or Not at All"

> **Paradise**
> The isolated, past-obsessed citizens of the all-black town of Ruby, Oklahoma, blame their problems on the women who live in "the Convent," a mansion just outside town: "They shoot the white girl first. With the rest they..."

Two reviews in *The New York Times*! A page-and-a-half in *The New York Times Book Review*! A seven-page cover story in *Time* magazine! Five pages in *The New Yorker*! Two pages in *Essence*! An

hour TV interview with Charlie Rose! A 20-minute rap with Ed Bradley on *60 Minutes*! In January 1998, reviews of (or articles about) *Paradise* appeared in nearly every magazine and newspaper in the United States.

What did all the reviews say?

Well, they were so mixed you wondered if the critics had read the same book! *Paradise* was murdered in one review and gloriously praised in another. It was called TM's most accessible book in one review and her most difficult in another. Two leading critics even disagreed on the subject of the book's opening line ("They shoot the white girl first.").

Bottom Line: Few of the first wave of reviewers really knew what was going on in the novel. *Paradise* may have been one of the most fascinating works of fiction ever written—and it was!—but most people didn't get it.

Oprah and TM's Later Works

During the six years Toni Morrison spent writing *Paradise*, the African American TV host and media mogul Oprah Winfrey took up TM as a kind of sacred cause. Oprah promoted TM's books, featured her on the *Oprah Winfrey Show*, and co-produced a film of *Beloved* in 1998. Oprah had been nominated for an Academy Award for her portrayal of Sofia in the 1985 film version of Alice Walker's *The Color Purple*, so it was not unreasonable of her to cast herself in the role of Sethe in *Beloved*. Well-intentioned as it was, the movie seemed to discourage more book readers than it attracted ... but don't let that stop you! Beloved is one of the triumphs of modern literature.

Toni Morrison's next novel—*Love*—appeared six years after *Paradise*, in 2003.

In 2008, TM published *A Mercy*.

Four years later, in 2012, she published *Home*.

And in 2015, the relentlessly prolific Morrison published *God Help the Child*, her eleventh novel. We will discuss TM's four later works together at the end of this book. Each of them takes TM in a different direction, expanding her themes—sometimes in direct opposition to her earlier work. Each of the later works has long stretches of great power and beauty, to be sure, but it would be premature to compare them to *Beloved* or *Song of Solomon*. There are moments in each of the books when you feel as if Morrison has come out of the novel and is speaking directly to you.

Morrison has also written the libretti (lyrics) for two operas: *Margaret Garner* (2005, music by Richard Danielpour), based on the same historical character that inspired *Beloved*; and the interactive musical narrative *Desdemona* (2011). Morrison's Desdemona, the victim in Shakespeare's *Othello*, is allowed to "answer back" to Othello (and Shakespeare!). Desdemona and the other female characters, invisible in Shakespeare's drama, are given voices in this unique production.

In addition to her novels, essays, stage plays and operas, Toni Morrison co-wrote books for children with her younger son, Slade, a painter and musician who died on December 22, 2010, at age 45.

Q: Is there anything we should know about TM's novels before reading them?

A: Ideally, you should read Toni Morrison's novels without coaching. Realistically, many people feel intimidated when they try to read "literary" novels without a bit of help. If you have never read a Morrison novel in its entirety and would like to try one on your own (don't tell the Literary Police!) read *Song of Solomon* first. It is one of the most readable literary novels by anyone, ever. That said, if you know a little bit about TM's goals and stylistic idiosyncrasies before starting, you will gain a deeper understanding of her work.

Forget about what I say in an interview—it might be anything— but trust the tale and start with that.

—Toni Morrison,
Bryn Mawr Alumnae Bulletin, 1980

HER WORK *Reinventing the Novel*

One thing Toni Morrison asks of her readers is to meet her books on their own terms. She wants us to understand her standards and her goals. But what are they? Morrison's overarching goal is to write the kind of book she'd like to read—a uniquely African American version of the novel. She would say, trying not to offend earlier black writers, that the novels that had been written previously by black people (especially men) were essentially "Eurocentric" novels *about* black people. So what would a true African Americanized novel be like for her? Morrison identifies 11 characteristics:

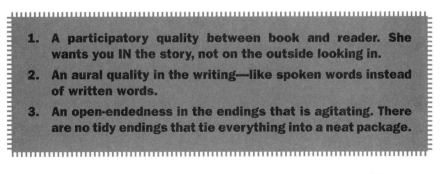

1. **A participatory quality between book and reader. She wants you IN the story, not on the outside looking in.**

2. **An aural quality in the writing—like spoken words instead of written words.**

3. **An open-endedness in the endings that is agitating. There are no tidy endings that tie everything into a neat package.**

4. An acceptance of and ability to detect differences—don't *homogenize* everything.

5. Acknowledgment of a broader cosmology and system of logic—one that includes magic and mystery and listens to the body.

6. A functional as well as an aesthetic quality. A jazz funeral march, for example, isn't *just* music; it is "functional" in the sense that it honors the dead and connects the living to their ancestors. (We'll look at other examples in Morrison's novels.)

7. An obligation to bear witness.

8. Serves as a conduit for the *ancestor*.

9. Use of humor that is often ironic.

10. An achieved clarity or epiphany and a tendency to be prophetic.

11. Writing that takes her people through the pain and denial of their racially haunted history to a healing zone.

Should You Judge Morrison's Novels on Her Terms ... Or Your Own?

Listen with an open mind to what TM and others have to say about her books. You should have a clear understanding of what she's trying to accomplish—and then forget everybody's terms, rules, and theories (including hers) and read the books with an open mind. Nine times out of ten, whether you love a novel or not will have nothing to do with the theory you vote for. Judge her books according to your own sense of beauty, logic, and meaning.

On the other hand, if TM's mission to create a uniquely African American novel makes you worry that her books may be less enjoyable or less beautiful to non-black readers ... nothing could be further from the truth! Morrison's books will thrill, irritate, and sanctify anyone who gives them a chance. And if she does succeed in creating a truly African American novel—like jazz, a truly African American music—people of every color will have insights and ecstasies they never had before.

This Book and its Approach

Toni Morrison For Beginners examines TM's novels from the perspective of what the critics have said about them, what TM herself has said about them, and what *this* author has felt about them. It would have been safer to quote only Toni Morrison and the literary critics—but that would have been a cop out. Why? In a 1981 interview, Charles Ruas asked Morrison a simple question: "How would you like us to read your novels?" Her answer posed a direct challenge:

> *I would like to put the reader into the position of being naked and vulnerable. Let him make up his mind about what he likes and what he thinks and what happened based on the very intimate acquaintance with the people in the book.*

In other words, Morrison wants us to drop our defenses and make up our own minds based on the relationships we develop with her characters. She *demands* a personal response.

That being the case, this book challenges both TM's critics and her disciples by offering different viewpoints on her work. As an introduction to her writing, of course, it also presents the conventional viewpoint. Beyond that, this book tries to explain what novelists do and how novels work for the general reader—the real nuts and bolts. Finally, it attempts to clarify what Morrison does so that aspiring novelists can try to apply it to their work. (Good luck with that!)

Like TM's writing, this book attaches particular value to three qualities: HUMOR, complete HONESTY, and SPOKEN English.

Spoken English? Yes, Toni Morrison makes a point of writing her novels in *spoken* English, as opposed to formal *written* English. She wants to convey the feeling that we are sitting across the table having a cup of coffee with whomever is "telling" her novel. So let's try to analyze her books in the same spirit. That also calls for:

HUMOR: Toni Morrison is in grave danger of being treated like a sacred cow. Definite mistake. This is serious stuff, but let's keep a sense of humor.

HONESTY: If you aren't certain you want a completely honest book on Toni Morrison, try another one!

The approach here is straightforward: Toni Morrison is the author of 11 novels of varying quality. Three or four of them are among the best in the world, one or two are klunkers, and the rest lie somewhere in between. This book focuses a great deal of attention on the three novels generally considered her finest: *The Bluest Eye, Song of Solomon,* and *Beloved*. Three other novels—*Sula, Tar Baby* and *Jazz*—have huge followings of passionate supporters, and—in the opinion of this author—*Paradise* is one of the most subversively brilliant books ever written.

For those of you who are new to TM's novels, let's take notice of a few things that will help you enjoy and understand her books.

A Few Things to Look Out For...
NAMES. Although she is sometimes as unsubtle as Charles Dickens when it comes to naming, Morrison doesn't name anyone or anything casually. She

names neighborhoods (The Bottom), streets (Not Doctor Street), and houses (124) with wit or foreboding. And her characters have startlingly beautiful Biblical names (First Corinthians), impersonal "generic" names (Son, Old Man), cartoon names (Chicken Little), ironic names (President Lincoln for a horse), and names out of Roman history or Greek mythology. TM's novels are filled with hidden treasures, many of which are connected to names.

The device points up a brutal truth of history: every black American whose ancestors were taken from Africa by force has been robbed of his or her family name. That was no accident. Wipe out a person's identity and you enslave their spirit. Your name and your family name are badges of identity. The slave-traders did everything they could to remove these badges (breaking up families, tribes, and language groups) leaving African Americans as a people in search of identity, even upon attaining their freedom.

HUMOR. Most discussions of Toni Morrison's work sound as if they were taking place in church. That's too bad, because all that reverence is liable to rob her writing of one of its great pleasures: it can be *funny!*

In *Song of Solomon,* Mrs. Baines' opinion of a "Negro" in business, Mr. Smith's suicide note, and the beauty-parlor lady's assessment of Milkman's and Hagar's relationship all are hilarious, ridiculous, sad, grim. In *Sula,* virtually everything One Legged Eva says is tilted in some brilliant comic way. Even in *Beloved,* after all that anguish, one stupid little joke reaffirms life.

So screw the reverence. Relax and let Morrison's humor shine through.

An OLD-FASHIONED Quality. Toni Morrison is variously known as a poetic, black, American, female, Faulknerian, magical realist writer, but one of the most satisfying things about her novels is that, in many ways, they are very old fashioned. Modern novels tend to be spare, economical, streamlined; modern authors often aspire to be a tape recorder or video camera, with no opinions, no thoughts, no digressions, and no dialogue over six words long.

Toni Morrison's novels tend to have too much of everything: too many characters, too many digressions, too much symbolism, too many flowery descriptions. Some of her novels are flawed by the most rigid standards of novel writing, but even then they are satisfying in ways that most modern novels are not. If the modern novel is like tasteful, ergonomically designed plastic furniture, a Morrison novel is substantial and ornate, made of four-inch thick

oak with fat, colorful pillows covered with clashing patterns, trimmed with red velvet fringes, and carved animal claws for feet—elegance and bad taste side by side.

STRADDLING HISTORY. Nearly every TM novel has elements that seem blatantly incongruent, as if she put a frog's head on an elephant. There may be a dozen different narrators (suggesting post-Faulkner modernism), but one of the narrators will be the author lecturing her readers (a technique scorned since Henry Fielding used it in the early 18th century). Or she'll give us a squirt of dialogue so real and racy that you think she tape-recorded it in a neighborhood somewhere ...

then she'll veer off into some hyper-poetic description that makes 19th century ladies sound like Ernest Hemingway. *("What's she serve for dinner—meatloaf and old socks?")*

It's like jazz critic Martin Gayford describing the music of legendary bassist/composer Charles Mingus: *"Mingus straddled history."* His music reached backward into jazz's past and forward into jazz's future, while completely ignoring—or "straddling"— jazz's present. In the same way, Toni Morrison's writing straddles history. She's as old-fashioned as Fielding and Dickens, as modern as Faulkner and Joyce—and she ignores damn near everything in between.

Morrison writes like a person on a sacred mission. In her words—

Our past was appropriated. I am one of the people who has to reappropriate it.

"It wasn't that easy being a little black girl in this country—it was rough. The psychological tricks you have to play in order to get through—and nobody said how it felt to be that."

—Toni Morrison

THE BLUEST EYE
(1970)

We recall why Toni Morrison began to write during the winter of 1967—she was out of work, depressed, and living in a place where she had no friends. But how did she choose the subject of her first novel? Or that unique writing style?

Her reasons had much to do with what she perceived as a gaping hole in Western literature. Westerners are justifiably proud of their literature—century upon century of some of the finest writing in the world. But imagine for a moment what that great wall of books feels like to a writer of color. To many black writers, Western literature is like a long Woody Allen movie: There's a lot of great stuff in there ... but where'd they put the black people?

Almost more tragic than the literal absence of black people in Western literature, in Morrison's view, was the fact that the black Americans whose books she had read (mostly men: Richard Wright, Ralph Ellison, and James Baldwin) seemed as if they were writing to a white audience, explaining things about black culture that they would never have to explain to her if they were sitting around over coffee. In the simplest terms, Morrison wanted to write a book about black people, in the language of black people, without having to look over her shoulder to explain her world to white people. One example she gives is the opening narrative of *The Bluest Eye*:

"Quiet as it's kept, there were no marigolds in the fall of 1941." To white people, "Quiet as it's kept" means ... "Quiet as it's kept." ...

Although there had been black women writers before her—she'd heard of Zora Neale Hurston, Lorraine Hansberry, and Gwendolyn Brooks—Morrison knew very little about them; they weren't being taught in the universities. So, setting out to write *The Bluest Eye*, Morrison felt that she was alone in wanting to express the world of the black people she'd grown up with. Above all, she wanted to talk about the people who were always in the background—like little girls. Toni wondered if she was the only person in the world who thought it was important to tell their story.

During the winter of 1967, Martin Luther King, Jr. and his co-workers were marching to desegregate the South, TM's former student, Stokely Carmichael, was raising hell as a leader of the Student Nonviolent Coordinating Committee, and everywhere you turned people of color were talking with pride about Black Power. But Toni Morrison wasn't buying it: "Whatever was going on, was not about me," she later said. "Nobody was going to tell me that it had been that easy. That all I needed was a slogan: 'Black is Beautiful.' It wasn't that easy being a little black girl in this country—it was rough."

Perhaps nothing hammered home what it meant to be "a little black girl in this country" more than a study that made headlines in the 1960s. A group of little black girls were shown drawings of other girls of varying color and asked to rate them. The children proved highly discriminating, picking up the most subtle differences in eye, hair, and skin color and arranging the pictures in a near-perfect sequence of light to dark. They were also consistent. In nearly every case, the little black girls rated the blondest, lightest-skinned, bluest-eyed girls as the prettiest, smartest, nicest, best little girls in the world.

Not long after that, race riots broke out in nearly every major city in America. And a new novel appeared, called *The Bluest Eye*. It had a few flaws, which gave you an excuse to ignore it if you couldn't handle what it said.

Correction: It didn't *say*—it *sang!*

The Image

If you take away all the detours, digressions, flashbacks, meditations on nature, pontifications on human nature, and writing so outrageously beautiful you want to kiss the page—if you remove all that and cut to the heart of the novel— *The Bluest Eye* is the story of Pecola Breedlove. No!—it's not the *story* of Pecola Breedlove, it's the *image* of Pecola Breedlove, an 11-year-old black girl who thinks her life would be perfect if only she had blue eyes.

The Story or the Book?

In a Toni Morrison novel, there's a big difference between the story and the book. The story can be summarized in two pages, but you still won't have a solid idea of what the book is about. *The Bluest Eye* is the story of three black schoolgirls growing up in 1940s Ohio— the sisters Claudia and Frieda MacTeer and their friend Pecola Breedlove. Claudia and Frieda's parents are strict, protective, and when they have time—which isn't often—loving. Pecola is ignored by her mother and abused by her father. Claudia, who tells much of the story, is a strong-willed eight-year-old black girl who can't stand the sight of little blond-haired, blue-eyed dolls. When she's given one for Christmas, her reaction cuts through the pretense:

"What was I supposed to do with it? Pretend I was its mother?"

She rips the doll to pieces, trying to discover what it is that everyone seems to find so lovable. The strong-minded Claudia can't stand the sight of the child movie star Shirley Temple, with her golden curls and baby-blue eyes. But 11-year-old Pecola idolizes Shirley Temple, drinks milk out of Claudia's Shirley Temple cup, and loves eating Mary Janes, the epoxy-like candies with the Shirley Temple clone on the wrapper. Pecola is lonely and sad. Her classmates tease her, telling her she is ugly, or sing-songing at her that her father's a drunk who sleeps naked.

Pecola, clueless to the war raging inside her, thinks that her life would be perfect if only she could have blue eyes. In one especially poignant scene earlier that day, Pecola had begun to menstruate. Neither she nor Claudia had the vaguest notion what that meant, but Frieda, who was a couple years older, did know:

That night, in bed, the three of us lay still. We were full of awe and respect for Pecola. Lying next to a real person who was ministratin' was somehow sacred. She was different from us now—grown-up like. She, herself, felt the distance but refused to lord it over us.

The scene that follows is tender, beautiful, and wise.

The THEME of the novel is strong, clear, and important:
Every black person in America is forced to struggle against a standard of beauty—as, by implication, most everything else, from goodness to worthiness for love—that is almost exactly the opposite of what they are... and the consequences can be deadly.

The novel suggests that the oppressive standard of Beauty peddled by movies and advertisements ravages white self-esteem as well...but it isn't just a matter of degree. Low self-esteem is an entirely different creature than self-hate.

But not for long. Pecola is raped by her drunken father and becomes pregnant with his child. As her pregnancy begins to show, instead of being sympathetic, her mother beats her and forbids her to go to school. When the baby is born prematurely and dies, Pecola loses her grip on reality. Desperate and confused, she visits a West Indian preacher called Soaphead Church to see if he can give her blue eyes. Soaphead, an unscrupulous creep who almost believes in his own "miracles," tells Pecola that God will give her blue eyes, but that she'll be the only one who can see them. By the end of the book Pecola is talking to an imaginary friend, asking if her eyes are the bluest of all.

That's the Story,
Now Let's Discuss the Book

A young black girl wants blue eyes, is raped by her father, goes crazy and dies. The story is certainly compelling, but it doesn't begin to suggest the power of the novel. It's the *form* of the novel—the way the story is told, the way the pieces are arranged, and what that arrangement implies—that generates its power.

If you aren't used to "experimental novels," the structure of *The Bluest Eye* might shake you up a little at first. (TM denies she was an experimental novelist, but in 1970 every novelist tried new approaches.) *The Bluest Eye* has three different beginnings. The first beginning is a slice out of one of those Dick-and-Jane books that so many of us learned to read with.

> *Here is the house. It is green and white. It has a red door. It is very pretty. Here is the family. Mother, Father, Dick, and Jane live in the green and white house. They are very happy.*

> *–First lines of The Bluest Eye*

The Dick-and-Jane primer makes several points (without mentioning them directly) before you know what hit you: every child in America grows up on Dick and Jane (or used to) and compares herself to Dick and Jane (who, in case you haven't noticed, are blond-haired, blue-eyed, and as white as it gets). So what happens if you can't stop measuring yourself against Dick and Jane?

The mild version is lack of self-esteem. The medium version is self-hate. The queen-sized version is Pecola Breedlove. By page two of the novel, the soul-shrinking Dick-and-Jane story has degenerated into chaos. The letters run together into one, long, ugly, meaningless, word—

> **"...willplaywithjanetheywillplayagoodgameplayjaneplay"**

This lasts only a few lines, and you don't have to read it to get the point. What Morrison manages to pull off in little more than a page is to "tell" the story of her entire novel in microcosm.

The second beginning is a one-page "gossip" in which Claudia (now a grown woman looking back on the story) gives just enough info for us to beg her to tell the rest. (It's as if you're sitting there over coffee, *listening* to the story, not reading it.) Most novels are essentially mysteries—you read to the end to find out what happens. That's not the case with *The Bluest Eye*. Claudia tells us the punch line on the first real page of the book:

> **Quiet as it's kept, there were no marigolds in the fall of 1941. We thought, at the time, that it was because Pecola was having her father's baby that the marigolds did not grow.**

LINEAR

Most novels, movies, and plays are linear. They proceed in a straight line: somebody wants something; they try to get it; they overcome one obstacle, which causes another; they overcome (or don't) that obstacle ... and so on, until they do (or don't) get what they want. The End.

But by the time we're being told the story (several years after the fact), Pecola, her baby, and her father all are dead. We also know that the story took place between Autumn 1940 and Autumn 1941. Since we already know *what* happened, we read the book to the end to find out *why* ... or, since why is difficult to handle, *how*.

The third beginning of *The Bluest Eye*—the "regular" story—begins on page three. The novel is divided into sections that correspond to the seasons, beginning with Autumn. Morrison's novels never forget their connection to nature, the seasons, and the past. As Barbara Christian wrote in an essay titled "The Contemporary Fables of Toni Morrison": "Wind and fire, robins as a plague in the spring, marigolds that won't sprout, are as much characterizations in her novels as the human beings who people them."

In each season that follows, grown-up Claudia introduces the action, time, place, and characters and sets the tone for the corresponding scenes. She speaks as "we," referring to herself and her sister—and in a very important sense, speaks for *us*. (Remember, one of TM's goals is to bring us into the novel, to make us participants instead of mere observers.)

Each chapter begins with a piece of the Dick-and-Jane primer, usually in contrast to the story that follows (e.g., comparing Dick-and-Jane's "pretty house" with Pecola's shabby house.) TM likes to use Contrasting Pairs and other kinds of Doubling.

Writers often work in Twos or Pairs so they can compare and contrast. The most common version is CONTRASTING pairs (Jekyll and Hyde, night and day, good and evil). Some contrasting pairs in *The Bluest Eye*: Dick-and-Jane fantasy and Pecola's reality; Pecola buys into white standard of beauty and Claudia fights it; Pecola's drab house and Geraldine's tidy house; Pecola and Shirley Temple. RELATED TERMS: *twinning, Doppelganger*

After Claudia's section ends, the next section begins with a few run-together words from Dick-and-Jane. Then the story is told by an omniscient (all-knowing) narrator who can go backward and forward in time and can jump in and out of anyone's consciousness. In these sections, we learn the backgrounds of Mr. and Mrs. Breedlove, Geraldine, Soaphead, etc.

Most books have a likable character you can "identify with"— here that's Claudia. Each season begins with Claudia telling us what that season means to her and how it affected Pecola's situation. Since this is Pecola's story, why doesn't TM have Pecola tell it herself? The problem is, if Pecola had enough self-awareness to tell her story, there would be no story! She would understand that judging herself by white standards of beauty is something to resist, not accept. Claudia and Frieda have been subjected to the same deadly standard of beauty as Pecola, but they resist it.

What about Cholly, Pecola's father? In TM's view, Cholly's

rape of his daughter was a twisted attempt at love, distorted by violence and expressed in violence. (If that strikes you as *too damn easy on him*, you're right!—but realize how Morrison has enticed you *into* the novel and made you grouch about characters as if they were people you know!)

Thus ends what we might call the Idealized Version of *The Bluest Eye*. For that, credit is due to Barbara Christian and her brilliant essay. Not only has she put her finger on the Idealized Design of the novel, but she's taken everything that might be considered flawed in the book and turned it into a virtue.

Other critics, such as Michael Awkward in "'The Evil of Fulfillment': Scapegoating and Narration in *The Bluest Eye*," mirror what early black scholar W.E.B. Du Bois called the "double-consciousness" of the Afro-American. (A black person living in a white country has to live with "two minds"—his own and the white man's—if he has any interest in survival. As Awkward sees it, "An exploration of Du Boissian double consciousness is at the center of the narrative events depicted in *The Bluest Eye*."

What Did the Critics Say?

For the most part, if they didn't like the book, they didn't bother reviewing it. Most of the reviewers had something good to say and something not so good, but there were generally more plusses than minuses...

> *She reveals herself, when she shucks the fuzziness born of flights of poetic imagery, as a writer of considerable power and tenderness, someone who can cast back to the living, bleeding heart of childhood and capture it on paper.*
>
> **–Haskel Frankel, The New York Times Book Review**

> *Morrison places the story in a frame of the bland white words of a conventional school "reader"—surely an unnecessary and unsubtle irony. She permits herself an occasional false or bombastic line. None of this matters, though, beside her real and greatly promising achievement: to write truly (and sometimes very beautifully) of every generation of blacks."*
>
> **–L.E. Sissman, The New Yorker**

And she got at least one review to die for:

J. LEONARD

> [She writes] a prose so precise, so faithful to speech and so charged with pain and wonder that the novel becomes pure poetry.
>
> –John Leonard,
> The New York Times

What Did Toni Morrison Say About It?

In a conversation with Jane Bakerman…

I thought in The Bluest Eye that I was writing about beauty, miracles, and self-images, about the way in which people can hurt each other about whether or not one is beautiful.

In a conversation with Anna Koenen…

Koenen: You seem suspicious of romantic feelings, like when you say in The Bluest Eye that the idea of romantic love is one of the most dangerous ideas which exist.

Morrison: [W]ho wants it, romantic love? The women who would want it are precisely the kind of women I would never like to be. It's a complicity between master and servant.

And in a conversation with Robert Stepto, she confides that she wrote Cholly straight through but got stuck when she came to Pauline. At that point, she says…

I didn't know what to write or how. And I sort of copped out anyway in the book because I used two voices, hers and the author's. There were certain things she couldn't know and I had to come in. And there were certain things the author would say that I wanted in her language—so there were ... two voices, which I had regarded as a way to do something second-best.

The Truth, the Whole Truth ...

The Bluest Eye is built around a great idea. It has an unforgettable image at its center. It has a theme of great moral importance. It has a beautiful cyclic design, fairly interesting characters, and some of the finest line-to-line writing you'll ever see. But it was Toni Morrison's first novel, and like every writer's first novel, it contains mishandlings and "amateurisms." Morrison has written some of the best novels in the English language and her best work is breathtaking, but she did not come into the world a fully formed novelist, and it is an insult to her best work to pretend that she did. Even worse, it plays a dirty trick on the thousands of writers who imitate everything she does, including her mistakes and amateurisms.

Two of Morrison's primary goals—a sense of intimacy (that feeling of sitting over coffee listening to a real person tell you the story) and writing that has the heartbeat of spoken language—work in such close combination that it's often impossible to distinguish one from the other. A fair amount of the time, TM pulls off the combination beautifully. When it's good, it's so good that when the flow is interrupted, you feel like you stepped into a hole.

There are two ways in which TM undermines the illusion of real people talking intimately in *The Bluest Eye*:

- **Using the wrong-sized language**

- **Using an overcomplicated assortment of narrators**

Wrong-Sized Language

If any aspect of the writing kills the illusion of real people in intimate conversation, it is that so much of the book is told in language that the characters (including the narrators) simply would not use. It hurts most where Morrison has worked hard to build wonderful effects and combine them into something as successful and moving as the night the three girls lay in bed after Pecola had her first period. Suddenly a lady that is supposed to be the grown-up Claudia pipes up in language fit for finishing school. Regardless of who or what she is, her high-falutin' words destroy every illusion of reality, intimacy, and real people engaged in real talk.

To be blunt, there are sections in *The Bluest Eye* where the language is so tight-assed that it's hard to imagine *anyone* using it! The most schoolmarmish line in the book is given to poor little Claudia, an intense eight-year-old child who is dying to rip a blond doll apart **"to see of what it was made."** Some lady with blue hair in a bun and eyeglasses on a chain may have said that once, but it seems unlikely any eight-year-old in the world has ever uttered those words. After Morrison, with patience and skill, creates this fascinating, headstrong child doing something so real and meaningful that we are drawn into her world, the narrator drops the line like an F-bomb in church: *to see of what it was made.* BAM—just that quick, we are jolted out of the reality of the novel.

In TM's defense, *The Bluest Eye* was her first novel. Contrast that with *Beloved*, which is told in language that is never fancier than the characters it describes, yet manages to create a range of emotions most of us can barely imagine.

Jumble of Narrators

Imagine you're Toni Morrison's ideal reader. You're sitting across

the table from the storyteller (probably a young Claudia) just as TM wants you to, sipping coffee and just dyin' for some nasty graveyard gossip—when the person you're sitting across from switches from young Claudia to old Claudia (or at least you think so, because you don't know much about her). Old Claudia says a few words, but then the person sitting across the table from you switches
to Pecola. Then she becomes Polly, who turns into Cholly. Cholly gives way to Soaphead, and Soaphead disappears to make room this Supermama who seems to be a cross between God, Sigmund Freud, and Toni Morrison! While some critics suggest that TM told *The Bluest Eye* from two viewpoints (Du Bois's "double consciousness"), in fact the novel has a dozen Consciousnesses! And in case the sheer number of narrators didn't squelch the intimacy Morrison sought, she added the kiss of death: the Cosmic Narrator.

The Cosmic Narrator (a godlike dude who knows everything about everybody and zooms through time and space, in one person's head and out the other) massacres the illusion of real people rapping over a cup of coffee and slaughters the sense of reality: *I was sitting there having coffee with the Cosmic Narrator, who told me the thoughts of 27 people at the same time!?*

Toni Morrison has a gift for inspiring people to become writers, so her novelistic techniques have an impact beyond that of pure literature. Aspiring writers should know this: mishandling of point of view is cited by many publishers and editors as the primary reason they reject novels. Any critic who ignores TM's mishandling of narrators in *The Bluest Eye* is playing a dirty trick on aspiring writers.

Morrison was a great *writer* the moment she hit the scene, but it took her several years to become a great *novelist*. Some critics overpraised Morrison's handling of multiple narrators in *The Bluest Eye* by comparing them to Faulkner. Not so.

How to Sabotage Your Own Book

One of the surest ways to guarantee that many people will NOT finish reading your novel is to digress a lot. Better yet, make those digressions long and "poetic." Long poetic digressions bring your story to a screeching halt. Toni Morrison digresses a lot. This is surely one of the main reasons that even people who love her work often leave a couple of her books half-read.

But the truth is, TM's digressions in *The Bluest Eye* contain some of the most beautiful writing in the book (if not the English language). So even if her digressions drive you up a wall, try to get over it and enjoy them for all they're worth! Even if it took her a few years to become a great *novelist*, Toni Morrison was a great *writer* from the minute she hit the scene. She had to be to get away with all those digressions!

BOTTOM LINE: Does any image convey the soul-destroying the impact of racism more powerfully than a black child praying for blue eyes? It's hard to think of one.

I thought of Sula *as a cracked mirror, fragments and pieces we have to see independently and put together.*
—Toni Morrison

Let us do evil, that good may come.
—Romans 3:8

SULA
(1973)

As we recall from Toni Morrison's bio, her second novel, *Sula*, was created out of a feeling that black women relate to each other in a different way than white women do. Perceptive critics like Barbara Christian and Robert Stepto felt that *Sula* was a natural progression from *The Bluest Eye*. TM lent credence to that notion when she said that it was natural to wonder what little girls like Claudia and Frieda are like when they grow up.

Sula has a large cast of the wackiest, weirdest, most wonderful characters you've ever seen, especially the supporting cast. Let's meet them before getting to the main story. Note that each character—including a neighborhood!—has a story of her or his own.

A FEW MAJOR MINOR CHARACTERS

The Bottom—Only TM could treat a neighborhood as one of the characters. The Bottom is a struggling, all-black neighborhood in which everybody knows each other and their business.

Shadrack—He came back from World War I shell shocked—"permanently astonished"—did time in a Vet's hospital, and invented National Suicide Day.

One Legged Eva—Sula's grandmother: "Fewer than nine people in town remembered when Eva had two legs, and her oldest child, Hannah, was not one of them."

Hannah—Eva's daughter; Sula's mother. She'd have sex with anyone but she was very choosy about where she slept.

The Three Deweys—One Legged Eva took in stray children and named them by the way they looked. She looked the first child over and said, "Well look at Dewey. My my mymymy." Awhile later she sent for a kid who kept falling off the porch ... and named him Dewey, too.

Tar Baby—One Legged Eva's tenant. The neighborhood said he was half white, but "Eva said he was all white." He had pale white skin and yellow hair, so naturally Eva called him Tar Baby.

Ajax—A "twenty-one-year-old pool haunt of sinister beauty" envied by men of all shoe sizes for his "magnificently foul mouth."

You get the idea: wacky, weird, and wonderful.

A Quick Look at the Story

Set in the "squinchy little town" of Medallion, Ohio, between 1919 and 1965, *Sula* is the story of two black women, Nel Wright and Sula Peace. They met at the age of 12, both "wishbone thin and easy-assed," both friendless except for each other, and both determined to explore everything in the world.

On the way home from school, four white boys knock Nel around. She avoids them after that, but one day Sula insists that they walk past the boys' hangout. When the boys approach, Sula takes out a knife and cuts off the tip of her finger. She looks at the boys and says quietly, "If I can do that to myself, what you suppose I'll do to you?"

One day Nel and Sula are playing down by the river. Sula is swinging a young boy around in a circle, when suddenly he slips from her hands and swoops into the water. He drowns. Nel and Sula know they're responsible but don't tell anyone. At the boy's funeral, Nel remains expressionless while Sula cries uncontrollably. Standing together a safe distance from the boy's grave, they hold hands in a tight clench, then walk home. A few years later, Sula leaves town in search of the "experimental life." Nel marries a dude named Jude and settles into a life of housewifing.

Ten years later—in 1937, the year Medallion suffered a plague of robins—Sula comes back to town. At Eva's house, four dead robins lie on the sidewalk. Sula pushes them into the grass with her toe. One-legged-Eva sees Sula at the door and says,

"I might have knowed them birds meant something. Where's your coat?"

About a minute after she finishes unpacking, Sula steals Nel's husband and puts Eva in an old folks' home. In no time at all, everyone in town hates her. The townspeople begin to define their lives in contrast to hers—"cherish their husbands and wives, protect their children, repair their homes and in general band together against the devil in their midst."

Sula dies young out of sheer orneriness, but she dies beautifully:

A crease of fear touched her breast, for any second there was sure to be a violent explosion in her brain, a gasping for breath. Then she realized that there was not going to be any pain. She was not breathing because she didn't have to. Her body did not need oxygen. She was dead.

Sula felt her face smiling. "Well, I'll be damned," she thought, "it didn't even hurt. Wait'll I tell Nel."

Years after she dies, in a flash of insight that puts everything in perspective, Nel sees that her friendship with Sula transcends everything. As the book ends, Nel hears Sula's voice blowing through the treetops near the old cemetery and realizes that all the years she thought she was missing her husband, she was actually missing her friend.

And the loss pressed down on her chest and came up in her throat.
"We was girls together," she said as though explaining something.
"O Lord, Sula," she cried, "girl, girl girlgirlgirl."

What the Critics Had to Say

DR. HORTENSE SPILLERS

Toni Morrison's Sula is a rebel idea, both for her creator and for Morrison's audience. .... [Sula] is, to my mind, the single most important eruption of black women's writing in our era.

–Hortense J. Spillers,
"A Hateful Passion, A Lost Love"

> *The heroine, Sula, grows up in a household pulsing with larger-than-life people... Her cherished friend, Nel, the local goody-goody, plays perfect counterpoint to Sula's intense, life-grabbing insistence on freedom.*
>
> As the author of frequent criticism and social commentary, Morrison has shown herself someone of considerable strength and skill in confronting current realities, and it's frustrating that the qualities which distinguish her novels are not combined with the stinging immediacy, the urgency, of her nonfiction.
>
> —Sarah Blackburn,
> *The New York Times Book Review*

> *In Morrison's narrative of a unique female friendship, Sula and Nel initially discover their own essences and begin to grow through their reciprocal connection; each girl seems to have ... what the other lacks.*
>
> —Roberta Rubenstein,
> "Pariahs and Community"

What Morrison Had to Say

With Robert Stepto (1976)...

> [O]ne can never really define good and evil. Sometimes good looks like evil; sometimes evil looks like good—you never really know what it is.

> [If Nel and Sula] they had been one person, I suppose they would have been a rather marvelous person. But each one lacked something that the other had.

With Anna Koenen (1980)...

> What I really wanted to say about the friendship between Nel and Sula was that if you really do have a friend, a real other, another person that complements your life, you should stay with him or her.

OK, fair enough. But let's go back to Morrison's quote about ignoring interviews.

> Forget about what I say in an interview—it might be anything—but trust the tale and start with that.

And that—trusting the tale—raises a few serious questions about *Sula*!

The Jive About Sula's Character

If you didn't have Morrison explaining that Sula only *appears* to be a self-absorbed brat but is actually the standard bearer of some super new morality where good looks like evil and vice-versa, you would never think so. Sula is brutal!

Part Two: Novel or Theory About a Novel?

Sula is like two separate books. Part One is the best-written half of a novel you'll ever read. Part Two almost isn't a novel at all. It's as if the main characters have left town and in their place are sociological descriptions of why they are the way they are:

> *The first experience [her mother saying that she loved Sula but didn't like her] taught her that there was no other that you could count on; the second [Chicken Little's drowning] that there was no self to count on either. She had no center, no speck around which to grow.*

Then TM tells us that Sula should have been an artist, but that nobody ever gave her the blah blah blah. *Please.* Even in fiction—especially in fiction—*saying* so doesn't make it so. Where's the evidence? Sula went away for ten years of "experimental life"—she could have painted! (Not to mention the fact that we already read that coulda-been-an-artist stuff about Pauline in *The Bluest Eye*.) Sula went away for ten years to put together an interesting self ... and when she came back, she was less interesting than her mother and nowhere near as interesting as old One Legged Eva. (Now *there's* someone who challenged conventional morality.)

Skip and Tell (Not Show)

One of TM's oddest choices in Part Two is her choice of which scenes/ events to "dramatize" and which to skip. She skips the ten years of Sula's absence ... interesting strategy. Then she skips right from Jude saying that Sula fascinates the mind but doesn't attract the body to Jude and Sula doing something ostensibly sexual. That could have been *very* interesting, but the "poetic" description of sex that fills the next several pages doesn't have much to do with the real thing. Toni Morrison, who can sum up a lifetime in 50 words, spends a dozen pages on abstract hogwash that *pretends* to be about sex.

And some reviewer or teacher may tell you that Sula's badness makes the townspeople good. OK fine, but when you read the book you may not be convinced. That's because TM doesn't *show* us that Sula's badness makes the townspeople good, she just announces it—she *tells* us. Nice theory, but nothing *happens* before our eyes to make the point.

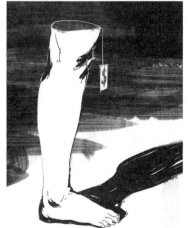

TELLING vs. SHOWING

In a sense, a story writer has only two options: either TELL you what happened, or SHOW you what happened (dramatize or present in a real scene). Virtually every story (novel, movie, or play) has a bit of both. The usual approach is to *tell the least important things and show the most important ones.*

Take the *New Testament*, for example: We are told in a sentence or two that Jesus spent the years between ages 12 and 30 preparing himself for the last three years of his life. Then we are *shown* those last three years in great detail.

The more extraordinary the events, the more important it is to show them. If the authors of the *New Testament* had described Jesus' more-or-less average life before 30 in great detail, then polished off his last three years in a sentence or two, there'd be no such thing as Christianity.

Real or Surreal?

Part One of *Sula* is surrealistic, fantastic; Part Two is more realistic. That poses a problem for the reader: How do I judge the events and people in Part Two? Do I judge them by the wonderful, whacko, surrealistic standards of

Part One (where a woman can sell her leg, make three individuals identical by calling them Dewey, and burn her son to death for his own good) ... Or do I judge them by regular, everyday standards where burning your son to death is pretty damn evil?

A Few Things to Note

- TM ventures two off-the-wall but very interesting theories:

  White people try to obliterate Evil; Black people accept Evil as part of life.

  The presence of Evil can cause Good. (See the quote from the Bible at the top of this chapter.)

- The "Doubling" strategies discussed in *The Bluest Eye* also lie at the heart of *Sula*:

  Nel and Sula go from a Similar Pair to a Contrasting Pair.

  Sula and Nel can also be looked at as incomplete halves of a whole. As TM said, if you put them together, they'd make a great person.

- "Funny" isn't a term you normally associate with Toni Morrison's writing, but Part One of *Sula* is hilarious—even if many reviews focused only on the grimness (e.g., Chicken Little's drowning) and others found it downright horrible. More than most books, *Sula* horrifies some people and tickles the hell out of others. The humor lies in recognizing that the truly bizarre people—especially One Legged Eva—are not realistic characters but surreal ones; metaphors, not mere people.

- There's one long section in Part One that you may find uncomfortable: the humiliation of Nel's mother, Helene. There is a similar but worse humiliation scene in *The Bluest Eye*, where Cholly goes looking for his father and shits all over himself. Any honest accounting of TM's "recurring themes" would have to include shit and humiliation.

- It may be cheating to look ahead to TM's next novel, which is largely about the importance of names, but it seems remarkably insensitive for Toni Morrison to name the little kid who drowned "Chicken Little," reducing him to a nitwit in a cartoon.

- One of the things that may bother you in TM's early novels is that she seems to force her characters into whatever ending she originally outlined, even though the characters seem to be going in a different direction. Sometimes she seems too controlling, and you find yourself rooting for the characters to fight back and assert themselves.

All that said, to be fair to Toni Morrison—and to better understand her book—we should look at TM's novel in light of her own standards. How does *Sula* fare against TM's own list of 11 goals?

1. A participatory quality between book and reader?

It's a chatty book for sure, but the chat would be more intimate if it were told by one person instead of a whole bunch.

2. An aural quality in the writing?

Spectacularly so! The writing, especially in Part One, is super-condensed spoken poetry. TM had not yet eliminated adverbs (softly, loudly, etc.) in *The Bluest Eye,* but she has in *Sula.*

3. An agitating, open-ended ending?

Sort of. Great book and very good ending, but they don't exactly match.

4. An acceptance of and keen ability to detect subtle differences?

This one could be a recipe for racism. (Every racist in the world is proud of his "ability to detect subtle differences.") Feel free to judge for yourself.

5. Acknowledgment of a broader cosmology and system of logic?

Yes, but it's small potatoes, rigged, and as unsubtle as a "plague of robins."

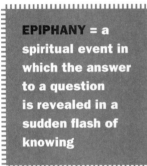

EPIPHANY = a spiritual event in which the answer to a question is revealed in a sudden flash of knowing

6. A functional as well as an aesthetic quality?

Yes, it's functional in a didactic sense (i.e., it "sells" a moral point-of-view).

7. An obligation to bear witness?

No, not yet. (That comes in her later work)

8. Serves as a conduit for the "ancestor"?

No. (Same as above).

9. Uses of humor that are frequently ironic?

Yes, on nearly every page of Part One!

10. An achieved clarity or epiphany and a tendency to be prophetic

See for yourself. (Damn right it's personal!)

11. A novel that would take her people through the pain and denial of their racially haunted history to a healing zone.

No, not yet. (That, too, will come in her later work.)

And the language...

Dear God, her language! Most people live in a world filled with objects, and words are invented to name those objects. Morrison lives in a world where God created Words ... and some time later, objects were created to fit the words. In Morrison's world, the beginning of the Bible isn't metaphorical, it's literal: "In the beginning was the Word..."

After the first half of *Sula*, you may well feel that Toni Morrison is the greatest line-to-line writer in the English language today. Most great writers are great at either the fancy stuff or the simple stuff; Morrison is magnificent at both. There is at least one line in *Sula* that has the elemental purity of the best in the Bible:

They spoke, for they were full and needed to say.

It's a line, like others in the book, that deserves to be sung, not just read aloud. Then light a candle or a stick of incense as a gesture of appreciation for the existence of such a writer.

Can't nobody fly with all that shit. Wanna fly, you got to give up the shit that weighs you down.

—Guitar, *Song of Solomon*

I wish I'd a knowed more people. I would of loved 'em all.

—Pilate's dying words,
Song of Solomon

SONG OF SOLOMON
(1977)

Toni Morrison's previous novels, *The Bluest Eye* and *Sula,* had attracted a great deal of attention largely because of their strong female characters. Instead of playing it safe and cranking out another "women's novel," Toni Morrison decided to write "a novel informed by the male spirit." That wasn't the only new ground it broke. Instead of being a neighborhood novel like her two previous books, it was a Tonimorrisonized generational novel. And instead of ending with monumental sadness, like her other books, it ends on a note of hope, redemption, and perhaps even spiritual transcendence.

It was ironic that Morrison should write what may be her most readable and life-affirming novel at a time when her personal life was so difficult. She had money problems. Her oldest son, now a

teenager, was a handful. And her father had died. As TM worked on her new novel, she carried on long conversations with her father in her head. She needed his help to write this new book about men, their "attraction to violence," and "the driving forces behind them."

And what a book it was. She called it *Song of Solomon*, and it was one those rare creatures: both a work of art and a great read. It was so full of life that it spilled over the edges onto anyone who read it. *Song of Solomon* is more complex than TM's earlier books. The story is easier to explain if you know the characters. As we've come to expect from a Morrison novel, each character—man, woman, and street—has a story...

THE MAIN CHARACTERS

Mr. Smith—Insurance agent who tries to fly from "No Mercy" Hospital across Lake Superior.

Milkman (Macon Dead III, called Milkman by everyone but his parents)—If a novel is a kind of fictional biography in which the main character undergoes an important change, Milkman is that character. The novel covers Milkman from his birth (in 1931, the day after Mr. Smith's "takeoff") to age 32, when he apparently undergoes a spiritual transformation.

Macon Dead II (called Macon or Macon Jr.)—Ruth's husband, Milkman's father; a hard man who despises his wife, ignores his daughters, and after a hateful start, treats his son Milkman with great respect. He's a landlord whose only desire is to acquire things. Despite being cast in the role of bad guy, he's a fascinating character. The locals think he's exactly like a white man! In the immortal words of Mrs. Baines: *"A nigger in business is a terrible thing to see."*

Ruth (Foster) Dead—Macon's wife, Milkman's mother; a character you don't know whether to pity or despise. She's a victim (TM saves her greatest contempt for Victims), but finds her own poetry in one sentence—*"What harm did I do you on my knees?"* As a human being, Ruth isn't much; as a character in fiction, she's as good as it gets.

Dr. Foster—The (creepy) father of Ruth Dead; the only colored doctor in town until his death of (fairly) natural causes in 1921, some 14 years before the novel opens. Dr. Foster's story is recounted in a series of mini-stories that tell of the past.

Not Doctor Street—The city wouldn't name the street where Dr. Foster lived "Doctor Street" so the locals, not to be denied, refer to it as Not Doctor Street. Morrison invests it with so much personality that it would be a sin not to treat a street as a character.

Magdalene (Lena)—Milkman's sister, 14 years older

First Corinthians—Milkman's sister, 13 years older.

Macon Dead I ("old" Macon Dead; originally Jake)—Macon Jr.'s father, Milkman's grandfather; a proud man with a brutally ironic sense of humor—especially when it comes to names: his own, his daughter Pilate's, his farm's (Lincoln's Heaven), and his horse's (President Lincoln). He was killed when Macon Jr. and Pilate were youngsters. Since then he has been his daughter Pilate's mentor.

Pilate Dead—Macon Jr.'s sister, Milkman's aunt (and spiritual mother). She's just like any other woman who wears her name in a snuffbox earring, carries a sack of bones, raps with her dead father, loves life like a boxful of puppies, and don't take no shit.

Reba Dead—Pilate's dim-bulb daughter, lives from orgasm to orgasm, has great luck until she needs it.

Hagar Dead—Reba's daughter, Pilate's granddaughter, Milkman's lover.

Guitar Baines—Milkman's best friend, a shining star of a young man who undergoes transformations that some readers find highly implausible.

Circe—midwife who delivered Macon and watched Pilate birth herself. She helps Milkman unravel the family history

The Seven Days—a secret group of black men who avenge the deaths of innocent blacks.

The Story

Song of Solomon starts out as a kind of "generational-via-rearview-mirror novel." Its present tense begins in 1931, the day before Milkman is born, and ends with his spiritual liberation (and perhaps his death) at the age of 32. Counting excursions into the past—three generations of the Dead family—the story covers nearly a century.

The novel opens as Smith the insurance man prepares to fly from the roof of (No) Mercy Hospital clear to the other side of Lake Superior. Two days before, Smith had tacked a note on the door of his house declaring his intent to "fly." Mr. Smith was well-liked (though no one urged him not to jump!) and draws a decent crowd, including a pregnant woman and a lady who sings him a song.

Born at No Mercy Hospital the day after Smith's attempted flight, Milkman was a gifted child until the age of four, when he learned that people can't fly. Bummed out by that depressing revelation, he grows into a self-absorbed young man who floats through life, committed to nothing, excited by nothing, taking the easy way out of every situation. Milkman works for his landlord father (with very little enthusiasm) during the day and parties (with very little enthusiasm) every night.

Macon (Milkman's father) rents out apartments in the run-down black section (the Blood Bank, to locals) and in a fancy white neighborhood nearby. He's a real hard-ass who collects as much property and "things" as he can. As bad as he is to his tenants, Macon is infinitely worse to his wife, Ruth. (When you find out why, you won't exactly blame him.) He is intense about everything except his daughters, to whom he's indifferent. Macon tells Milkman why he detests his wife, but instead of appreciating his father's confidence, Milkman is irked because he's been burdened with a lot of crap about his mother. If Ruth were a bit more innocent and a little less creepy, she'd be a perfect victim; and the more you learn about her, the creepier she gets. When she tells Milkman her side of the story, he's no more sympathetic to her than he was to his father.

Milkman, who moves fast only when avoiding responsibility, spends more and more time with his friend Guitar Baines and with his mystical aunt Pilate, his father's estranged sister. Macon and Pilate had parted ways because of an argument 30-odd years earlier after their father was murdered in Pennsylvania. Although his father had forbidden him to see Pilate, Milkman and his energetic buddy Guitar first visited her when Milkman was 12 years old.

As they came closer and saw the brass box dangling from her ear, Milkman knew that what with the earring, the orange, and the angled black cloth, nothing ... could keep him from her.

Of course she was anything but pretty, yet he knew he could have watched her all day...

On the day Milkman met his aunt Pilate, he also met the beautiful rear end of her granddaughter Hagar. They became lovers when he was 17 and she was 22, and they remained lovers for years until he grew as bored with her as he was with everything else. Little by little, we learn that "old" Macon got his peculiar name when he told a drunk Union Army sergeant that he was from Macon, Georgia, and that his family was dead. Macon was such an ornery cuss that, for spite, he left the name as it was. He named his daughter by opening the Bible and putting his finger on a word that looked like a tree. He couldn't write, so he drew the word and showed it to Circe, the midwife. Circe told him he couldn't name his daughter "Pilate." Macon, who couldn't read, said, *"Like a riverboat pilot?"*

"No. Not like no riverboat pilot. Like a Christ-killer Pilate. You can't get much worse than that for a name. And a baby girl at that."

"That's where my finger went down at."

After old Macon was killed by some white men for his property, Macon, Jr. and Pilate thought the killers might do them next, so they hid in a nearby cave. When an old man wandered into the cave, jittery young Macon killed him. When Macon and Pilate discovered gold in the cave, he wanted to take it and she said it was wrong—and they went their separate ways. Macon eventually headed back to the cave, but the gold was gone. He figured that Pilate had taken it.

When Macon Jr. and Pilate met later, she admitted she'd gone back to the cave, but only to get the old dead man's bones. Her father, who visited her regularly, told her it was wrong to "just leave a body," so she went back to get the bones (which she still carries with her), but she said the gold was gone. Macon was certain she had the gold, so although he had been like a father to her for the first 12 years of her life, he hated her for the next 30. Pilate, barely into puberty when she and Macon split up, spent time in a lot of places. Sooner or later, she realized, someone would discover that she doesn't have a navel and people would treat her

The Story is One Thing, How it's Told is Another

The storytelling form in *Song of Solomon* is certainly unusual, but typical Toni Morrison: secondary characters are given nearly as much space as (and more interesting personalities than) the main character. If a new character enters the story (or an old one needs a new paint job), Morrison stops things cold (even though the hero might be suspended with one foot on a cliff and another in mid-air) to tell you about this minor character's parents and his one-eyed philosophical wino uncle and the time he got the measles from the preacher's daughter's music teacher's nephew. Morrison is like the FBI: She has a dossier on everyone.

like a freak. And so, with the help of her father—her mentor despite the fact that he had died—Pilate started from scratch...

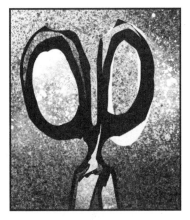

She threw away every assumption she had learned and began at zero. First off, she cut her hair. That was one thing she didn't have to think about any more. Then she tackled the problem of trying to decide how she wanted to live and what was valuable to her. When am I happy and when am I sad and what is the difference? What do I need to know to stay alive? What is true in the world? Throughout this ... one conviction crowned her efforts: since death held no terrors for her (she spoke often to the dead), she knew there was nothing to fear.

Meanwhile, back in the present tense...

Guitar confesses to Milkman that he is a member of The Seven Days, a secret organization that avenges the killing of innocent black people. Guitar, who seems to have undergone a psychological transformation since we last saw him, grouches Milkman out for not being "a serious person." After his parents had been kind enough to share their dirty laundry with him, Milkman had just about all the seriousness he could bear. Milkman can't take the pressure (*what* pressure?) and tells his dad he wants to get out of town and wants Macon to support him for a year or two. Macon tells his son about the gold he still thinks Pilate stole. That would solve Milk's problems and give Macon's fortune a nice boost.

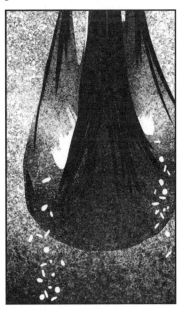

Meanwhile, Hagar is not handling Milkman's rejection very well. *"Must not be working out if she's trying to kill him,"* says one of the beauty parlor ladies.

Milkman and Guitar team up to get the gold. Pilate doesn't have it, so they decide that it must still be in the cave in Pennsylvania. Guitar wants to help look for the cave, but Milkman wants to do it alone. To locate the cave in Pennsylvania, Milkman first has to go to Virginia, where the family was from.

At the point when Milkman begins looking for the cave, the book becomes a "quest novel," like a man in search of the Holy Grail. As in a detective story, Milkman travels through Pennsylvania and Virginia, asking questions and piecing together clues. Along the way, he finds the easy friendship of people in one small town, offends a local in another town without knowing what he did wrong (even though it ends up in a fight), and goes hunting with some other guys who might be friendly or deadly, he's not sure which. He has a nice little two-night stand with a lady named Sweet. The words with which Toni Morrison describes it turn a list of innocuous behaviors ("she put salve on his face…") into a definition of love.

Guitar turns up, acting like he's had a lobotomy, trying to kill his former best friend. Milkman does not find gold, but he does find his family's history, both in fact and feeling. As he travels through the South, one of Milkman's clues to his background comes from the "Song of Solomon," a nursery rhyme he overhears children singing in a small Virginia town. The song is a lot like the one Milkman had heard Pilate sing when he was a child:

Sugarman done fly away
Sugarman done gone
Sugarman cut across the sky
Sugarman gone home.

But the kids in Virginia don't say "Sugarman." Instead they say "Solomon." Milkman realizes that the song is part of his own family history—the "Solomon" in the song is his great-grandfather, a slave who, according to legend, escaped bondage by flying back to Africa. The novel ends with… Nevermind, read it for yourself!

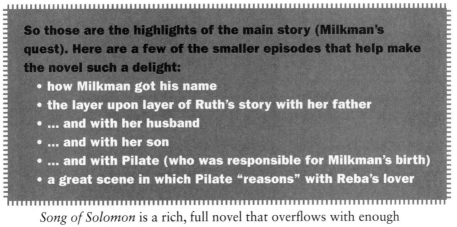

So those are the highlights of the main story (Milkman's quest). Here are a few of the smaller episodes that help make the novel such a delight:

- how Milkman got his name
- the layer upon layer of Ruth's story with her father
- ... and with her husband
- ... and with her son
- ... and with Pilate (who was responsible for Milkman's birth)
- a great scene in which Pilate "reasons" with Reba's lover

Song of Solomon is a rich, full novel that overflows with enough people and stories to keep most writers busy for two lifetimes. It had to be a great success. You don't often see a novel that's literary enough for the fancy-minded and so welcoming to anyone with enough interest to open it. That's all you had to do—the book is so readable it damn near reads itself for you.

How Did the Critics Like It?

A delight, full of lyrical variety and allusiveness ... peopled with an amazing collection of losers and fighters, innocents and murderers, followers of ghosts and followers of money, all of whom add to the pleasure of this exceptionally diverse novel.

–Neil Millar, *The Atlantic*

The "Song..." [in] the title of Toni Morrison's third novel is a variant of a well-known Gullah folktale about a group of African-born slaves who rose up one day from the field where they were working and flew back to Africa. In the novel, this tale becomes both the end of, and a metaphor for, the protagonist's identity quest.... In basing Milkman's identity quest on a folktale, Morrison calls attention to one of the central themes in all her fiction, the relationship between individual identity and community ... of the common experiences, beliefs, and values that identify a folk as a group.

–Susan L. Blake, "Folklore and Community in *Song of Solomon*"

What IS the Book About?

One thing that makes Toni Morrison's novels so much fun is that you can spend hours arguing with friends, classmates, teachers, and yourself about what you just read. What is the book about in a general sense? What is the book's main theme or point or meaning? What is it trying to tell us? As usual, we'll look at conventional views of the book first.

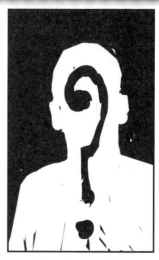

The one-line description of *Song of Solomon* is that it's the story of Milkman Dead's quest for identity. The two-line version, plus or minus a word, usually goes like this: Milkman, an aimless, self-absorbed young man, starts on a journey to find gold and finds something more important along the way: his family history. Obviously one of the main themes of the book is Milkman's quest for identity. In his case, part of the quest for identity is literal: he wants to find his name.

NAMING—The Best Way They Can

Naming, after all, is one of the great orchestral themes of Song of Solomon: If not for a Pilate and a Guitar, Macon (Milkman) Dead would not have learned to fly.

–John Leonard, The Nation

We talked about the fact that every black American whose ancestors were taken from Africa by force (over 90% of present-day African Americans) has been robbed of his or her original family name. Given that a name, especially a family name, is a badge of identity, finding his name was the natural first step in Milkman's quest for identity.

But like everything else in *Song of Solomon*, naming branches out in many directions. Old Macon named his animals, his farm, his daughter, and himself as if naming were an act of vengeance. "Down South" names were like street signs turned the wrong way: if you were one of the locals, you knew things by their right names; if you weren't, *too damn bad*. One of the best scenes on naming was between Milkman and Guitar. Their friendship is changing, hovering between trust and suspicion, and they sound like they're talking to each other from different rooms. In one conversation, Guitar gets fed up with Milkman's self-pity and self-absorption and tries to jolt him back to reality:

> **"What's your trouble? You don't like your name?"**
> **"No." Milkman let his head fall to the back of the booth. "No, I don't like my name."**
> **"Let me tell you something, baby. Niggers get their names the way they get everything else—the best way they can. The best way they can."**

Naming was the first step in Milkman's quest for identity. Flying was the last.

FLYING—Myth and Metaphor

When asked what *Song of Solomon* was about, Toni Morrison didn't equivocate:

> *It's about black people who could fly. That was always part of the folklore of my life; flying was one of our gifts. I don't care how silly it may seem. It was everywhere—people used to talk about it, it's in the spirituals and gospels.*
>
> **–Toni Morrison to Mel Watkins, 1977**

TM emphasized that this was not merely an Africanization of the Greek myth of Icarus. Though they have some things in common, this is a distinct and distinctly African myth. The best-known version comes from a Gullah folktale. (The Gullah are a people from the Sea Islands off the coast of South Carolina and Georgia. Blacks who lived there kept their African heritage more intact than at any other place in the Americas.) Milkman's flying is not just literal—it's a metaphor for his identity quest.

The myth of the Flying Africans in *Song of Solomon* would mark the first (but definitely not the last) time that Toni Morrison designed a novel around myth and folklore.

Ancestry and Community

Honoring one's ancestors, one of the foundations of African society, is also trademark of Toni Morrison's fiction, but she didn't deal with the issue until *Song of Solomon*. Characters like Pilate and Circe live, almost literally, in a community with their ancestors (Pilate talks constantly with her dead father), but Milkman starts out with no connection to anyone or anything. In the process of searching, however, he begins to feel a connection to the people around him. For the first time, he feels a bond to the community and even a bit of responsibility for it.

LOVE (or a Two-Night Stand)

Milkman learns so much in a very short time. He learns how to love somebody, nicely, tenderly, give something in return....

–Toni Morrison to Mel Watkins, 1977

She put salve on his face. He washed her hair. She sprinkled talcum on his feet. He straddled her behind and massaged her back. ...

–Song of Solomon

Maybe, when you write like Toni Morrison, your words are so beautiful they seduce you into thinking you can turn a two-night-stand into real love. There's love coming from all over *Song of Solomon*—but Milkman's two-nighter? Really?

This novel *reeks* with love, real love: Ruth's crazy father-love, Hagar's sad love, Pilate's universal love ... and all the love that comes right out of Morrison's words.

WORDS ... When the Language is Right

And sometimes, when the language is right ... I begin to react to the characters who say certain things. In Song *when Milkman's mother says to his father, "What harm have I done you on my knees?", then I loved her. I felt all kinds of chilling things. When the language fits and it's graceful and powerful like I've always remembered black people's language to be, I'm ecstatic.*

–Toni Morrison to Mel Watkins, 1977

Other TM novels have long stretches of wonderful writing, but *Song of Solomon* is Toni Morrison's most finely written book from cover to cover. Something about the language seems to celebrate life more than the others. And about that quote—do you feel the same way? Is the language right? Do you have to remind yourself that there really is no Ruth, no Pilate, no Macon ... only *words?* Is a scientist who creates life in test tubes any more miraculous than a writer who creates living human beings with *words?*

SYMBOLISM and Guitars

There is loads of everything in this novel, including symbolism. Said the author herself:

This man, Milkman, has to walk into the earth—the womb—in that cave, then he walks the surface of the earth and he can relate to its trees—that's all very maternal—then he can go into the water, which is untrustworthy, then he can bathe and jump into the water, then he can get to the air. ... Pilate is earth. Her brother is property.

–Toni Morrison to Anna Koenen, 1980

When a writer talks like that about her characters, she runs the risk of diminishing them. She may as well hang signs on them.

Pilate's house (with Reba and Hagar) is the Maternal Household where everyone is free and equal; Macon's house is the Paternal Household, arranged in a hierarchy from Boss to Invisible. Pilate is Milkman's Spiritual Mother, Ruth his Natural Mother. Ruth is Prisoner, Pilate is Free. Macon is a Taker, Pilate is a Nurturer. Flying is Freedom, Emotional/Spiritual Emancipation .

And Guitar? Guitar is ... what? Symbolic of a man with a different personality on every page?

Speaking of Guitar, there were two things people complained about in *Song of Solomon*—Guitar and the ending. Susan Lardner, writing in *The New Yorker*, expressed perfectly what many felt about Guitar:

> **"I have to admit having trouble figuring out the full purpose of ... Guitar. [H]is conversion from Milkman's closest friend ... into his nemesis [is] a puzzle to me."**

And you may be even more confused about The Seven Days than you are about Guitar. Guitar and Milkman talk, discuss, and argue about The Seven Days for a couple hundred pages, but you never quite know what to make of it. Who are these guys?

DEATH and Ambiguity

Pilate seemed to have found the right way to deal with everything, including death. She talked regularly to her father, her mentor, even though he had died years ago; she had no fear of death; she thought there was a good possibility that you don't have to die if you don't want to; she mourned the death of her daughter without restraint; and she gave her life for Milkman without hesitation.

But what about Milkman's death?

Death? *What* death?

Morrison told interviewers that she never believed that Milkman and Guitar would kill each other. She thought they would merely lock horns "like antelopes." But Morrison may have been the only person in the universe who thought they wouldn't kill each other. There was no suggestion of mere head-butting in the book—and a lot of people didn't love the ending.

> *Many readers decry ... the deliberate ambiguity of Morrison's conclusion.*
>
> **–Jan Furman, *Toni Morrison's Fiction***

From the Inside Out

If you try to read *Song of Solomon* the way TM said she wants us to read her books—to get inside the novel and be with the characters, instead of staying on the outside and looking in—you may come out with some insights different from those of the critics, or even Morrison herself. And in the case of this novel, it doesn't take much effort to climb inside and disappear.

So try it that way, and see what you think of these views...

About 400 years ago, William Shakespeare wrote two plays that he thought were about a historical king named Henry IV. In the process of writing about ol' Henry, Shakespeare created a secondary character called Falstaff. Most supporting characters know their place and stay in

the background where they belong. But this marvelously whacky knight Falstaff had a mind of his own. No matter how hard Shakespeare tried to shove him into the background, Falstaff, by the sheer power and beauty and life-loving force of his personality, stole the whole damned show.

Isn't that exactly what happened with Pilate?

Toni Morrison can tell us till her nose falls off that Milkman is the star of *Song of Solomon*, but it just ain't so. No matter what she intended, WE know—from the inside!—that Pilate is the heart, soul, and spiritual center of *Song of Solomon*.

By every meaningful definition of the term, Pilate is the main character. The minute she walked into the novel, the page lit up like God was shining a flashlight from behind. No matter how many critics, and TM herself, claimed that Milkman is the hero of the novel—*you* know that Pilate is its beating heart. She is the standard against which we judge the other characters and ourselves: an intuitive genius, a passionate humanist, a friend who will visit you even after you die; a mother who will protect you from a bad man without forgetting that the bad man has a mother too. Every time Pilate leaves the book, she leaves a hole no one else can fill. Whether or not she outgrew Morrison's original scheme for a book, Pilate emerges as its spiritual center and joins the ranks of great American fictional characters.

> **Q: If Pilate is the center of the book, does that mean Milkman isn't?**
>
> **A: No it doesn't. The book has two centers.**
>
> **Q: Why two centers?**
>
> **A: Because, functionally, *Song of Solomon* is two books: a Eurocentric novel set inside TM's first fully formed African American novel.**

Beware of Critics Bearing Gifts

One of the more surprising rave reviews of *Song of Solomon* came from Harold Bloom, perhaps the most prominent literary critic of the time. One of the most original and innovative critics in America, Bloom was nevertheless a conservative defender of the literary "canon," the so-called Greatest Books in the World—most of them written by Dead White Guys. Toni Morrison had spent her career publicly fighting against the canon and the kind of "Eurocentric novel" it epitomized. Indeed, Morrison's ideal of a truly African American novel was a systematic rejection of the Dead White Males and their rigid attachment to the Eurocentric novel. Bloom, who had not been a great fan of Morrison, now predicted that *Song of Solomon* was so good that one day it would be part of the canon. After comparing Morrison to Faulkner several times, Bloom kicks into professorspeak:

> Milkman Dead, the protagonist of Song of Solomon, is a true Faulknerian quester, driven by a metaphysical need for his true name, and for the transcendental folk-values that have been alienated from him. Milkman's search begins to find fulfillment only when he comes upon the appropriately named Circe, an aged black woman who incarnates a total rejection of all principles and standards that are not African. She sends him to his ancestral American village, where initially he is resented almost as though he were wholly contaminated by white culture. Later he undergoes a [radical] metamorphosis. There is nothing else in Morrison's work so magically strong (and indeed strongly magical) as Milkman's transformation. It is wholly persuasive.
>
> –Harold Bloom, *Contemporary Black American Fiction Writers*

Bloom's review, for all its self-magnifying positivity (*"Faulknerian quester"* indeed!), feels a little like a Trojan Horse. *Song of Solomon* is a sprawling, river-with-tributaries-branching-in-all-directions novel. It branches out into the mini-novels of Pilate and Macon, Old Macon's naming frenzy, Pilate's journey of self-discovery, Ruth and her strange father, Hagar trying to ice Milkman, Guitar and The Seven Days— and dozens of others that Bloom chooses not to see.

Why did Bloom focus ONLY on Milkman's "Faulknerian quest" and review it as if it were the entire novel? Smart cookie that he is, Bloom isolated Milkman's Quest because he recognized it as a perfect little Eurocentric novel-within-a-novel. By praising it, and *only* it, he shot a zinger at Morrison even as he praised her novel. (Like, "You can rant about the white-bread Eurocentric novel, honey, but it's the only thing worthy of note in your best book!")

All trash talking aside, don't overlook Bloom's point: the Milkman's Quest, isolated from the rest of the book, is a perfect example of the Eurocentric novel. And the point is a useful one. Being aware that it satisfies the "structural" demands of the Eurocentric novel actually helps us understand certain aspects of *Song of Solomon*.

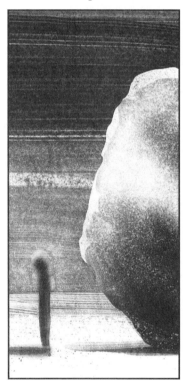

How so? Once you realize that Milkman's Quest is (among other things) a Eurocentric novel, things that didn't add up before suddenly make perfect sense: like Guitar and The Seven Days. All you have to know about the Euro-Novel are the bare essentials. Details will be provided as we go.

How Do We Explain Guitar?

Why did this bright young guy, Milkman's best friend, turn into a robotic madman and try to kill him? Was it for some deep psychological reason? No. Guitar went nuts because of the structure of the Eurocentric novel! It goes like this: If you look at the ingredients of the Euro-novel, you'll see that you need four things: 1) a Hero (in this case Milkman); 2) a McGuffin (cave, family history); 3) several fairly plausible Obstacles and; 4) one Last BIG Obstacle.

The Last Big Obstacle should be a person who's such a bad ass that the Hero will be the underdog. He should also be someone we know (it's cheating to bring in major players late in the book). But Milkman is in a strange town, hundreds of miles from home, badly in need of a Last BIG Obstacle, and none of the locals qualify for the job. So what do you do? You import one from home.

It should be someone we know well. Like Guitar. But if he's too sane and principled to shoot his best friend, then make him IN-sane and UN-principled! Any decent Eurocentric novel needs a Last Big Obstacle, and Guitar was going to be it—even if he had to be relocated and lobotomized. So how do you "modify" Guitar and turn him into a whacko assassin? You invent a group. What kind of group?

Any kind, so long as it has the following characteristics:

- It must have enough of a good side and a rational enough justification that we don't automatically write off anyone who joints it as totally nuts.

- It must be bad enough so that when Guitar does snap, it automatically stands as a sort of we-should-have-seen-it-coming "explanation"

> **RECIPE for the EUROCENTRIC NOVEL**
>
> 1. A Hero (Milkman) who REALLY wants something (gold, to find the cave, family history, etc.)
>
> 2. A "McGuffin"—dopey word Alfred Hitchcock used to indicate whatever the Hero is chasing: gold, a cave, family history, ticking time bomb, whatever. Hitchcock says they're interchangeable, but a suspense story needs at least one. In extreme cases, the Hero will kill to get the McGuffin—and die if he doesn't get it.
>
> 3. Obstacles—The Hero goes after the McGuffin, but some obstacle (local yokels, broken car, missing info) keeps him from getting it. He overcomes that obstacle, but then another obstacle gets in his way... and another...
>
> 4. Last BIG Obstacle (Guitar and gun)—The last and toughest obstacle of all. Either the Hero overcomes it and gets his McGuffin, or he loses it forever...

- **It must have guns. One of the Commandments for a well-made plot: "If you want to shoot somebody in Act 3, you have to put a gun on the table in Act 1."**

So while The Seven Days doesn't compute as a group of toxic avengers, it makes perfect sense as a fictional device invented to: a) give Guitar an excuse for his busted personality; b) provide a fairly plausible reason (orders from the group) for Guitar to ice Milkman (they thought he squealed on Henry Porter); and c) "put guns on the table" in Act 1.

A Fully Realized African American Novel

It wouldn't make sense to argue that TM has to actualize all characteristics of the African American novel in one book before you can say she pulled it off. By any fair measure, *Song of Solomon* stands as TM's (or any writer's) first fully realized African American novel. Judge for yourself, but she probably nailed 9 out of 11 of her stated goals:

- **The book is intimate.**
- **It reads better than spoken words—like music, in fact.**
- **It brings you in as a participant.**

- Pilate's wisdom brings clarity; the writing brings epiphany.

- It acknowledges a broader cosmology than the narrow scientific worldview.

- Honoring ancestors is one of the main themes: Pilate and Circe live with their ancestors (Pilate constantly talks with her father); Milkman's quest is essentially a search for his ancestors.

- There is a feast of ironic humor: the most obvious examples are the names "old" Macon gave his farm (Lincoln's Heaven), his horse (President Lincoln), etc.

- The book is functional in the sense that it means to teach you something: Pilate's list (*"she threw away every assumption she had learned and began at zero"*) and, some say, flying.

- The ending certainly agitated a lot of people (if not always in the way TM intended).

Song of Solomon meets every goal but two that Morrison had set for her Afro-American novel.

1) An obligation to bear witness.

2) A novel that would take her people through the pain and denial of their racially haunted history to a healing zone.

It would take Morrison another ten years to realize these last two goals. And she would do it with one of the most powerful books in modern American literature. But let's stay in *Song of Solomon,* which can really be viewed as *two* novels: an African America novel *and* a Eurocentric novel. If you look at it that way, Milkman is the center of one novel and Pilate the center of the other. (Or, if you prefer, Pilate's story is a subplot.)

Which one do *you* like more? Why?

Milkman and His Conversion

In all fairness to Milkman (after all, he's only a character in a novel), he really is dull compared to Pilate. Everyone who reads *Song of Solomon* remembers Pilate. Many remember Milkman, but few think he's anything special. One of the reasons Milkman has an underwhelming personality is that TM doesn't give him any good lines. One Legged Eva (in *Sula*) was an ornery old buzzard, but TM gave her such quirky words that she nearly stole the novel. If

Morrison had dressed Milkman in her Sunday language, she could have turned him into a true Hero. But no. As the novel stands, Milkdud was a boring young man who couldn't fly no matter what TM said about him.

Many novels, including *Song of Solomon*, aim to "convert" the hero (small h) to a "religion" or belief system of the author's choice. So maybe another reason it's so hard to get interested in Milkman is that the religion and his conversion aren't very convincing: Head to the small town where your grandparents lived, get to know the locals, and undergo an intense spiritual awakening. *That's it?* Due respect, but having a few beers, getting punched out, stomping around a cave, having a two-night stand with a local lady isn't likely to change your life—not Down South or anywhere else.

And the Quest itself is lame! There was no pressing need or compelling reason for Milkman to find his family's history, and he finds nothing earth-shattering in that history to justify all the hullaballoo. Milkman spends 200 pages chasing one of Hitchcock's McGuffins!

About that Flying

And the flying that lies at the symbolic heart of the novel? It's little more than a frame for the story—a minor and unconvincing one at that. The flying stuff, every hint and detail, takes up no more than five or ten pages. If there were no mention of flying at all, would *Song* be a significantly different book? Or a less beautiful one? Or if, at the end of the book, Milkman busts out in a big grin, gives Guitar a high-five, and says, "We know we could fly if we want to—we just don't want to!"—would that have hurt the book?

Probably not.

Still, even if the ending is unconvincing, the fact that Toni Morrison wrote a joyful one counts for a lot. If a book is a world in which the writer is God, wouldn't you rather have a God that allows life to end in a meaningful way rather than one who destroys her characters and blames it on "reality"?

And then there is the "other" novel. Pilate's novel. The first fully realized African American novel. It's hard to find words that capture the power of *Song of Solomon* and the character that lies at its true spiritual center. Whatever her other reservations, critic Susan Lardner (*New Yorker* magazine) finds the magnificence of *Song of Solomon* in one of those many smaller episodes that help make the book a triumph.

> *[I]n four pages that would have to be reprinted whole for proper quotation, Morrison describes Pilate bursting into a funeral service with a shout, shifting into a whisper, then a question, then two songs, and then speaking "conversationally" to each member of the congregation, her "words tossed like stones," we are told, "into a silent canyon."*
>
> *Suddenly, like an elephant who has just found his anger and lifts his trunk over the heads of the little men who want his teeth or his hide or his flesh or his amazing strength, Pilate trumpeted for the sky itself to hear, "And she was loved."*

The epiphany, the spiritual awakening, the transcendence ... they're all there.

> *I wish I'd a knowed more people.*
> *I would of loved 'em all.*
>
> —Pilate's dying words

The earth does not argue,
It is not pathetic, has no arrangements,
Does not scream, haste, persuade, threaten, promise,
Makes no discriminations, has no conceivable failures,
Closes nothing, refuses nothing, shuts nothing out.
          —Walt Whitman, "A Song of the Rolling Earth"

TAR BABY
(1981)

Most of us know the story of the Tar Baby, either from the folktales of Br'er Rabbit and Br'er Bear popularized by the white American writer Joel Chandler Harris in his Uncle Remus collection or from the 1946 Disney movie *Song of the South*, a feature-length cartoon in which birds and butterflies and all of nature sing. What many people may not know is that these stories were "borrowed" from African American culture without so much as a Thank You. Variations of Br'er Rabbit "trickster" tales were common in black communities all over the Americas. The stories had originated in West Africa and were brought to the New World by the men, women, and children who had been abducted into slavery. Separated from their homes, families, and native cultures, they adapted the stories to fit their new situation—powerlessness, humiliation, and physical abuse.

Br'er Rabbit wasn't some cute cracker cousin of Bugs Bunny; he always represented the slave. Not a lion or an elephant or some other powerful creature, but a rabbit. All he had going for him were his wits, but if he played his cards right...

The folktales and the character held particular fascination to Toni Morrison.

I use that old story because, despite its funny, happy ending, it used to frighten me. The story has a tar baby in it which is used by a white man to catch a rabbit. "Tar baby" is also a name, like nigger, that white people call black children, black girls. I found that there is a tar lady in African mythology. For me, the tar baby came to mean the black woman who could hold things together. The story was a point of departure to history and prophecy.

—Toni Morrison, Interview in *New Republic*, 1981

The Story: Generic Version

The second thing you notice about Morrison's *Tar Baby* is that you can read a description of the book and have no idea what the texture is like. (The first thing you notice in the opening pages is that it seems to have been written by someone else.) Summaries of the story generally begin by saying that it is set on a small, fictitious island in the Caribbean, Isles des Chevaliers, named after a group of mythical African horsemen. According to the legend Morrison provides in the book, the Africans had been brought to the island as slaves, managed to escape, and were said to be roaming the hills on horseback.

Against this mythical backdrop, Morrison tells a modern love story: Jadine, a beautiful, black model, is the niece of Sydney and

Ondine Childs, longtime servants of a retired white millionaire named Valerian Street. Valerian, who lives on an estate on the island, has paid for Jadine's fancy French education and treats her with great respect ... in stark contrast to the way he treats his much younger, ex-beauty queen wife Margaret.

One evening, Margaret discovers a raggedy intruder hiding in her bedroom closet. She is panic-stricken, but Valerian invites the intruder to dinner and a sleepover. At first, both Margaret and Jadine are afraid the man might rape or murder them, but—BAM!—Jadine and the man (called Son) fall in love.

During Christmas dinner, Son sets off an argument that ends up involving everyone in the household, shaking each of them out of their comfortable roles. The dark flip sides of their relationships are shown to be reeking with exploitation, mutual dependence, and complicity in unmentionably dirty deeds. The evening ends with Valerian rendered silent, Sydney and Ondine wondering if they still have jobs, and Margaret mumbling to the moon about her innocence.

Son and Jadine run off to New York City. Jadine loves it there, but Son finds it unbearable and eventually talks Jade into going with him to the tiny town where he grew up: Eloe, Florida. Jadine, who finds Eloe even more miserable than Son found New York, splits.

In the book's climactic scene, Son rapes Jadine, accuses her of being cut off from her "ancient properties," and tells her the story of the tar baby. Like the tar baby, she is something "made" by a white man. The novel ends with Son unsure whether he can (or wants to) break free from the hold of this beautiful woman—who, like the tar baby, has ensnared him--or whether he wants to join the band of mythical horsemen said to be tromping around the island.

What Did the Critics Say?

For the most part, *Tar Baby* got decent reviews. Still, it seemed that everyone who wrote about it had read a different book. Critic Claudia Tate described *Tar Baby* as a sort of racially stressed, symbolic Jackie Collins love story:

Morrison's latest novel, Tar Baby *(1981), is about the evolution of an intimate relationship between an unlikely couple. Jade, a jet-set fashion model, falls in love with a young vagrant only to become estranged soon thereafter. He is not discouraged by their breakup but pursues her with the hope of reconciliation. Through the use of elaborate symbol, Morrison suggests that reconciliation between the black man and the black woman can only occur when they mutually understand they are both victims of racial exploitation.*

In a book titled *Toni Morrison's Developing Class Consciousness* (2004), Dorothea Drummond Mbalia characterized *Tar Baby* as a political novel, starring a kind of Pan-African Che Guevera:

> *[I]n* Tar Baby *Morrison creates a revolutionary protagonist, Son.... Having discovered first the importance of knowing one's history and one's relationship to his people, Son commits himself to sharing this knowledge with other Africans. Thus, by struggling to politically educate Therese, Gideon, Sydney, Ondine, and, in particular, Jadine—symbols of the larger Pan-African society—Son becomes a disciple for African people, a modern-day revolutionary.*

Judith Wilson, interviewing TM for *Essence* magazine in 1981, was concerned that Morrison's new novel might be troubling to young, upwardly mobile black women. Wilson's questions underscored her unease:

> *Can women like Jadine, who have options Black women never had before, reconcile freedom with responsibilities—to elders, men, children?*
>
> *Isn't that asking for Superwoman?*
>
> *Jadine ... seems like the "heavy" in the battle between her and Son. Are you saying that women like her, who are privileged, with a college education and a lucrative career, should feel guilty about themselves in comparison with men who are poor like Son?*

As Ms. Wilson's questions indicate, the most passionate discussions were not about *Tar Baby* as a novel but about the conversations—or debates—that take place IN the novel between Jadine and Son.

If those two made love half as much as they talked, they would have had had 27 children before the novel was over. For now, let's just note that one of the things that instantly make *Tar Baby* feel so different from other Toni Morrison novels is the enormous amount of talk. Proportionally, *Tar Baby* has about three times as much dialogue as Morrison's other books.

The review by John Irving (author of *The World According to Garp* and other good novels) is quite complimentary, but he seemed to be more annoyed than he lets on when he compared TM's "old-fashioned authorial intrusions" to those of 18th century English writer Thomas Hardy, who stopped to lecture readers in the middle of his novels. When it came to TM's dialogue, however, Irving didn't waffle:

> Too much of the story is told through dialogue—and not only through the old couple's conversations. Their niece, Jadine, a super-educated Paris model who "made those white girls disappear right off the page," has a love affair with an escaped criminal, a poor, uneducated north Florida black. Jadine and her lover, Son, passionately debate the best way for blacks to be independent of the white man's world. Their arguments are lengthy and become tedious.
>
> –*The New York Times Book Review*, March 29, 1981

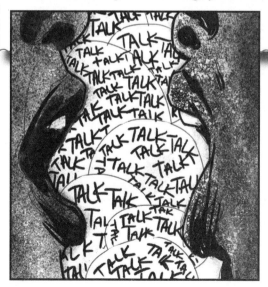

Despite all the advance hype, many readers felt that *Tar Baby* didn't measure up to TM's normal standards. It felt like something was missing. Even John Leonard, perhaps TM's most passionate advocate, couldn't fall in love with *Tar Baby*:

> **I fell off the truck with Tar Baby *(1981). It still seems overly didactic, somehow brittle, her only novel you can't sing...***
>
> –John Leonard, *The Nation*

But what did Aunt Remus herself have to say?

Toni Morrison Talks About *Tar Baby*

In a conversation with Thomas LeClair...

> *It's a love story, really; the tar baby is a black woman; the rabbit is a black man. He is determined to live in that briar patch. Do you think she would go into that briar patch with him? Well, that's what it's all about.*

In a conversation with Nellie McKay...

> *Many of the problems modern couples have are caused not so much by conflicting gender roles as by the other "differences" the culture offers. That is what the conflicts in Tar Baby are all about. Jadine and Son had no problems as far as men and women were concerned. They knew exactly what to do. But they had a problem about what work to do, when and where to do it, and where to live. These things hinged on what they felt about who they were, and what their responsibilities were in being black.*

So what do we make of all this? If *The Bluest Eye* showed us the devastating results of judging people by the way they look, and if *Song of Solomon* taught us the importance of naming, what are we supposed to do with a book in which people UN-ironically fall in love based entirely on looks and the hero and his father have generic names (Son and Old Man)? Could Toni Morrison have written a book as silly and shallow as *Tar Baby* seems to be *on the surface?* Or is there more to it?

Again, see for yourself. Don't read the hype—not from the critics, not from the author— read the novel! To repeat Morrison's own words: "Forget about what I say in an interview—it might be anything—but trust the tale and start with that."

The Real Story

Let's start with the epigraph. The quote at the front of a novel is like a fortune cookie that sums up the book's meaning or main theme in a few words. The epigraph in *Tar Baby* comes from the New Testament:

For it hath been declared unto me of you, my brethren, by them which are of the house of Chloe, that there are contentions among you.

—*First Corinthians* 1:11

OK, fine ... but what does it mean? First Corinthians is the first letter (or epistle) that St. Paul wrote to Christians in the Greek city of Corinth, famous for its sexual hanky panky. Paul was named Saul until being struck by a blinding flash of light and becoming a disciple of Jesus. But First Corinthians is not only a letter from Paul—it's also the name of one of the characters from Toni Morrison's *Song of Solomon*. And Chloe is Toni Morrison's given name. Why would TM use a quote "co-authored" by one of her own characters, with her own name in it, as the epigraph? Were her intentions serious, humorous, or somehow both?

As ever, Humor and Ambivalence are key to understanding: The "contentions among you" mentioned in the quote are, in fact, within Chloe.

Tar Baby begins and ends with what TM calls "parentheses"— brief descriptions of Son going to the island on a boat. The narrative within the parentheses begins with nature itself telling the story. Parrots and trees and clouds all talk, socialize, and have opinions. Everything in nature thinks, speaks, sings, and watches people destroy it. Your  first impression may be that the Nature Chorus sounds charmingly silly and Disneyfied. Or is it serious and mystical?

Let's give the author some credit. If the material seems to be cartoony, then it was *meant* to be cartoony. From this point of view, *Tar Baby* starts out as a cartoon chorus in which nature tells us what shitheads we've been for messing her up. It's a kind of a Greek chorus, via Walt Disney and Toni Morrison, that provides a running commentary on the action. It lasts only a page or two at the start but recurs throughout the book.

Unfortunately, a great start is followed by about 60 pages of well, misery—writing so bitchy and misanthropic you'll have to force yourself through it. Valerian, this above-it-all candy magnate sees a beauty queen on a parade float and marries her because she's pretty. Eye Candy. She's 20 years younger than him and so socially klutzy that you feel sorry for her—until the little bimbo refers to Sydney and Ondine as "Kingfish and Beulah." No matter how her husband treats her, she is a woman the reader is clearly not intended to love.

The hard part continues until the scene in which Margaret Eye Candy finds the tattered vagrant (Son) hiding in her closet. From that moment on, the book, while not up to TM's usual standards, is okay. It's easy to read ... even if it may seem superficial and shallow.

But wait! Consider another possibility. (If clouds can talk and rivers can cry, maybe we're dealing with a whole new set of rules.) What if you wanted to write a book that illustrated, demonstrated, and proved with the only means at your disposal—words—that the world without black men in it would be an ugly place, devoid of beauty and music and pleasure and tolerance? Perhaps the most brilliant and convincing strategy would be to begin the book without a black man and, to prove to us how necessary he is to beauty and pleasure and tolerance, write an extended narrative of misery, misanthropy, and empty talk. It's an interesting possibility, no?

In any event, the Bad Black Outlaw suddenly appears in Eye Candy's closet—**BAM!** She's scared witless and goes running to her husband, Valerian, named for a pink and white flower whose roots herbalists use to put you to sleep. Kingfish zooms upstairs with a gun to ice the intruder, whom Morrison refers to in the book as "literally, literally, the nigger in the woodpile"—an impolite image to be sure, but a cartoon nonetheless.

Noteworthy Detail: This Gentleman in the Woodpile, who had been hiding in the woods and starving for months, does not steal meat and potatoes or something that a real human being would eat. No way. This starving desperado steals designer water and chocolate bars.

The whole wonderful book is a cartoon!

Item: Remember when Ondine—Beulah—said that Jadine was so beautiful that her face in a magazine made those white girls fly right off the page? That wasn't a just metaphor—those white chicks literally flew off the page!

But it's Son's shower that takes the cake....

The night that all the nice people discover the Gentleman in the Woodpile, Margaret is so terrified that she doesn't sleep a wink; Jade is scared but not enough to miss her beauty sleep; Sydney sits awake all night with a pistol in his lap (no comment!). The following day, as Jadine and Margaret hide out in their rooms, putting their

hairdos together to figure out how to get rid of him—unbeknownst to them—the terrifying, dirt-crusted, dreadlocked Gentleman in the Woodpile that they thought was a rapist/murderer biding his time, takes a shower. A shower!

And the next time they saw the stranger he was so beautiful they forgot all about their plans.

This, dear reader, must rank as one of the most magical, metamorphistically cosmic showers in the history of fiction! Here's this tattered, hungry vagrant, uglier than a policeman's armpit, who takes a shower—just a shower—and **BAM!**, he's so gorgeous that brutal island jungles grow soft in his presence and blind chicks drive boats through treacherous waters!

He and Jadine take one look at each other and—**BAM!**—dreads over heels in love!

How was Son a cartoon character?

He might have survived the chocolate bars and the designer water. Maybe we could have forgotten the Mother of All Showers after 50 or a thousand pages. But this gentleman, considered by some a romantic hero and by others a revolutionary whose half of the dialogue thousands of people take life-and-death seriously, is presented as a man in harmony with nature. In contrast to Jadine's white-man taint, he is the unsullied, natural black man, undamaged by Western concepts of work and modern "civilized" existence. Son, in other words, is presented as some version of ... call him Ideal African Man With A Few Flaws.

So where does Ideal African Man With A Few Flaws want to take Jadine to wise her up and connect her to her "ancient properties"? To some ancestral Yoruba village? To a mountaintop in Kenya or a cave in Serengeti? Maybe a sacred waterfall in Haiti or an after-hours rib joint in Harlem where Diz and Bird had coffee? Hell no!

Ideal African Man With A Few Flaws wants to take his baby to Florida... Eloe, Florida.

If Son had any credibility at all, Eloe killed it. He may as well have taken Jadine to Toledo, Ohio. After all, one spiritual capital of the world is as good as another.

But Those *Words!*

Whatever flaws we may see in the characters or themes, we can't leave *Tar Baby* without a taste of Toni Morrison's traffic-stoppin' words:

She didn't want to have any more discussions in which the silences meant more than the words...

her sex life had become such a wreck it was downright interesting.

They refused loans at Household Finance, withheld unemployment checks and drivers' licenses, issued parking tickets and summonses. They jacked up meetings in board rooms, turned out luncheons, energized parties, redefined fashion, tipped scales, removed lids, cracked covers, and turned an entire telephone company into such a diamond head of hostility the company paid you for not talking to its operators. The manifesto was simple: "Talk shit. Take none."

"Oh, horseshit!" she said aloud. It couldn't be worth all this rumination, she thought, and stood up. The avocado tree standing by the side of the road heard her and, having really seen a horse's shit, thought she had probably misused the word.

The Bottom Line

The most polite assessment of *Tar Baby* is that it is the weakest of Toni Morrison's novels. That's no big deal: even the greatest writers write some klunkers. And a great book—like *Song of Solomon*, say—carries such force that it can be overpowering. Sometimes a writer has to burn down the house to get rid of what it left behind. For Toni Morrison, *Tar Baby* may have provided that sort of psychic cleansing—a necessary space before her next novel, *Beloved*.

Thus, *Tar Baby* can be seen as a vital transition between *Song of Solomon* and *Beloved*. A less-than-wonderful novel … but a perfect cleansing.

Denver picked at her fingernails.
"If it's still there, waiting, that
must mean that nothing ever dies."
Sethe looked right in Denver's face.
"Nothing ever does," she said.
*   –Beloved*

BELOVED
(1987)

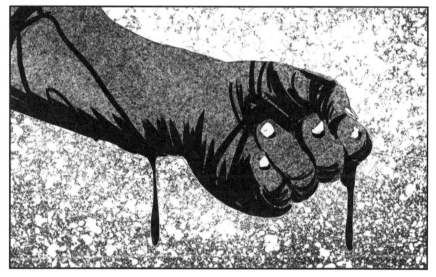

SPOILER ALERT!

In many of her novels, Toni Morrison reveals critical information in the first few pages, so it makes no difference if you know in advance. In *Beloved*, it does make a difference. Morrison structured *Beloved* as if the reader had no advance knowledge of either the novel's central tragedy or the identity of the title character. So if you haven't read *Beloved* and you want to experience it exactly as TM wrote it, don't read past this page.

On the Other Hand...

Of all Toni Morrison novels, *Beloved* may be the one that readers abandon most often because they have no idea what's going on or they feel intimidated by the book's "literary" style. As original and innovative as her first four novels were, *Beloved* is a whole other world, reaching levels of almost impossible beauty. It's a shame if people give up on the book simply because they are confused or intimidated by the literary technique. Part of the unique spell that this novel casts is a powerful need to share it! So to those of you who have started *Beloved* and given up, read this chapter! Here's what you need to appreciate the book deemed "the best American work of fiction of the past 25 years."

Background

In the early 1970s, while helping Spike Harris gather material for *The Black Book,* Morrison read an article she couldn't get off her mind. Titled "A Visit to the Slave Mother Who Killed Her Child," the article was about a slave named Margaret Garner who escaped from a Kentucky plantation in 1856 and fled with her four children to Ohio. When finally tracked down by her master's slavecatchers, Garner tried to kill her children so they couldn't be forced into slavery. Only one of the children died,

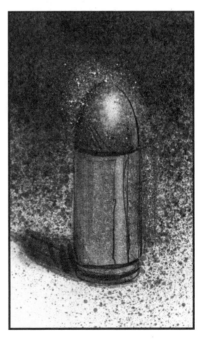

but Garner said she'd rather her children were dead than made slaves and "murdered by piecemeal." What struck Morrison about the story was that even after being imprisoned for the murder of her own child, Garner believed she had done the right thing.

One of the characteristics of Morrison's genius is that she sees things in a unique way. Her take on Garner's suffering is a perfect example. It was, TM said, "a despair quite new to me but so deep it had no passion at all and elicited no tears."

For years after reading the account, Toni Morrison wanted to write Margaret Garner's story—but it refused to happen. Morrison almost decided that the story couldn't be written, but in the end she found the power by surrendering to that of the Garner family: "In the end, I had to rely on the resilience and power of the characters— if they could live it all of their lives, I could write it."

How do you tell the story of a woman who kills her own child? What can you say that isn't shrunk into insignificance by the terrifying logic of the act itself?

Help came as well from the lead character in a play Morrison had written in 1983, called *Dreaming Emmett* (1983). Based on a true story, the play was about a teenager named Emmett Till who had been shot in the head and thrown into a river for whistling at a white woman. In Morrison's play, Emmett came back from the dead to speak for himself. She would elevate that technique to a new level in *Beloved*.

THE KEYS

If you keep two facts in mind—

One, *Beloved* (the novel) is based on the true story of Margaret Garner, the mother who killed her child;

Two, Beloved (the character) is the dead child returned to Sethe (as if they have some unfinished business between them)—

then the novel, despite all its complexity, is not confusing. Toni Morrison has rendered the changes in time and place with such elegant logic that the story unfolds as clearly as if it were told chronologically.

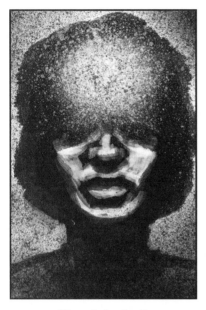

The Story

The year is 1873. The house, known by locals as "124," is located on 124 Bluestone Road on the outskirts of Cincinnati. Sethe (the Margaret Garner character), formerly a slave on a Kentucky plantation called Sweet Home, has been free for 18 years. Eight years earlier, Sethe's two sons had run away from home. Two months after that, her mother-in-law, Baby Suggs, died. By the time the novel opens, only Sethe and her 18-year-old daughter Denver—along with the ghost of a dead baby girl—live in 124.

"For a baby she throws a powerful spell," said Denver.
"No more powerful than the way I loved her," [Sethe replies.]

Sethe flashes back 18 years to the time she traded a stone carver ten minutes of sex to carve the word "Beloved" on her baby's headstone. We aren't told how the baby died; we learn the details only in flashbacks. Throughout the novel, events in real time are interrupted by memory—but it's reluctant memory. Whereas other flashback novels resurrect the past, *Beloved* is an attempt to forget it. We get only what leaks through the cracks.

When the novel opens, the Civil War has been over for eight years and all the characters are trying to forget everything about slavery. Even Sethe tries to close off the past, but her "devious" brain lets though chunks of memory: *"Boys hanging from the most beautiful sycamores in the world."* Sweet Home, that hateful place, looked so beautiful it made her wonder if hell was pretty too.

On the tail-end of that memory, Paul D, another former slave from Sweet Home, turns up at 124. But when Paul tries to enter the house, he's stopped in his tracks by *a pool of red and undulating light.* He remarks on the feeling of evil, to which Sethe responds, *"It's not evil, just sad."* Sethe asks Paul D to stick around—they (and we) have 18 years of catching up to do—and Paul chases the ghost away. A few days later, a beautiful woman—about the age Sethe's baby would have been if she'd lived—comes to the house. She calls herself Beloved. The novel that bears her name and tells her story shuttles back and forth in time, filling in the past, moving through the present, and connecting one to the other.

With apologies to the author for telling the story in a different sequence, perhaps the clearest way to recount the events from this pivot point between past and future—the arrival of Paul D and Beloved—is to go back 30 years and do the "catching-up" all at once.

In about 1840, a pair of "nice" slave owners had a plantation in Kentucky called Sweet Home. Paul D, his two brothers (Paul A and Paul F), and Sixo were slaves at Sweet Home when Baby Suggs, a limping old woman, arrived with her lastborn child, a son named Halle. The Garners treat the slaves with uncommon respect; they call the men "men," value their opinions, and let them carry guns. Once they set foot outside Sweet Home, however, the slaves are "boys" to everyone else.

Garner does not free any of his slaves, but he does allow Halle to buy his mother's freedom. Baby Suggs wonders why he bothers to do so—what can a crippled old woman do with freedom? But when she walks through Cincinnati a free woman, she can't believe that *"Halle, who had never drawn one free breath, knew that there was nothing like it in the world."*

Sethe, 13-years-old, arrives at Sweet Home to replace Baby Suggs. The three Pauls and Halle all have their eyes on her. (Sixo, the rebel, has his own woman). Sethe marries Halle and has two sons, Howard and Buglar. In about 1853, after Mr. Garner dies, Mrs. Garner sells Paul F and lives for two years on the proceeds. Then she frets that she can't run Sweet Home "alone" (though she still has Sethe, Halle, Paul D, Paul A, and Sixo!), so she sends for her brother Schoolteacher and his two nephews to help her. Unlike Mr. Garner, who treated his slaves like semi-human beings, Schoolteacher beats them, measures their body parts to support his racist eugenic ideas, and makes "scholarly" lists of their human and animal characteristics.

The novel asks some hard questions about slavery, such as:

How do you go about living "freely" after an experience that negates the very concept of self?

The complete erasure of identity has never been so fully dis-expressed as in the list of zeros that add up to Baby Suggs' life. Garner, the "nice" slave master, asks her name:
"What do you call yourself?"
"Nothing," she said. "I don't call myself nothing."
Without knowing if her children are dead or alive, what they looked like or where they might be buried, Baby Suggs realizes that she knows even less about herself:

Could she sing? Was she pretty? Was she a good friend? Could she have been a loving mother? A faithful wife? Have I got a sister and does she favor me? If my mother knew me would she like me?

During the first year of Schoolteacher's reign, Sethe's daughter Beloved is born. Sethe and the men can't bear Schoolteacher's cruelty and talk about escape. With three children and pregnant with her fourth, Sethe can't bear the thought that her children might be sold—so she runs away. She gets her children

safely to Baby Suggs, but she is caught and returned to Sweet Home by the nephews. One holds her down while the other sucks the milk from her breast—a violation worse than rape in her mind. She tells Mrs. Garner, but the nephews find out and beat her bloody.

Sethe sees Paul D strapped into a three-spoke neck-collar and looks away to spare him shame. (Eighteen years later, when he turns up at her house, Sethe will learn from Paul D that her husband Halle had been hiding in the loft while Sethe was being molested. The last time Paul D saw Halle, he had gone mad from what was done to his wife while he hid, unable—or in his own mind, *unwilling*—to intervene.)

Sethe and Halle had planned to escape separately and meet later, but Halle never shows up. Sethe fears he is dead. Pregnant and exhausted, but driven by the idea that her baby needs her milk, she runs away, then collapses. She is saved by Amy Denver, a young white indentured servant on the run to Boston. Amy nurses Sethe halfway back to health, helps her deliver her baby (named Denver in honor of the weird young woman), and zooms off.

Sethe makes it to Baby Suggs' house outside Cincinnati. Her sons are healthy and happy, and the baby Beloved is already climbing stairs. Baby Suggs, made ecstatic and holy by freedom, has become a spiritual leader whose love of life, self, and the whole blessed world transform those around her. (Baby Suggs is one of the glories of the novel—someone we could all go to school on—until the world caves in on her.)

Sethe, ecstatic about being united with her children, can't believe how much you can love people when you're free. Then, after 28 days of freedom, she sees Schoolteacher riding on horseback into Baby Suggs' yard. Sethe collects *"every bit of life she had made, all the parts of her that were precious and fine and beautiful"*—her children—and takes them into the shed. She manages to kill only one, Beloved, before Baby Suggs and the others stop her. Sethe is taken away to jail, nursing her baby Denver, as drops of Beloved's blood drip into her milk.

Released from prison after a few months, Sethe is shunned by her neighbors but doesn't give a damn what they think. The only person who has the right to question her is the baby whose throat she had cut out of pure love.

CAST OF CHARACTERS

Sethe—Beloved's and Denver's mother; Baby Suggs' daughter-in-law; 14 years old when she marries Halle; 20 when she escapes from Sweet Home; 38 when the novel opens in 1873.

Beloved—Sethe's daughter, killed at age 2, returns as a 20-year-old woman to confront, love, and ravage her mother.

Denver—Sethe's 18 year-old recluse daughter.

Baby Suggs—Sethe's mother-in-law; Halle's mother; spiritual leader of the free community.

Halle—Sethe's husband; Baby Suggs' son; bought Baby Suggs' freedom; so gentle and giving he was doomed under slavery.

Paul D—One of the male slaves from Sweet Home; becomes Sethe's lover.

Sweet Home—Kentucky plantation where Sethe and the others worked as slaves.

Mr. Garner—owner of Sweet Home; "nice" slave master.

Mrs. Garner—after he dies, she becomes an invalid and sends for her brother-in-law, "Schoolteacher," to run Sweet Home.

Schoolteacher—brutal slavemaster; a prototypical "scientific" racist.

Schoolteacher's Nephews—two sadistic young morons who molest Sethe.

Sixo—The bravest and baddest of the male slaves, almost cartoonishly heroic.

Paul A and Paul F—Paul D's brothers; Paul F is sold and Paul A is hanged.

Thirty-Mile-Woman—Sixo's lover; the mother of "Seveno."

Amy Denver—flaky young white indentured servant who helps Sethe deliver Denver.

Stamp Paid—an older former slave who runs the ferry boat and survived a brutal life without becoming brutal.

Ella—member of the Underground Railroad; she goes from moral to moralistic and back again.

Underground Railroad—an informal network of safe-houses, routes, and people that help runaway slaves and free blacks escape to Canada.

The Bodwins—brother and sister white abolitionists—Quakers, not crackers!

Janey Wagon—free black woman; works for the Bodwins and specializes in gossip.

Lady Jones—Denver's schoolteacher.

Howard and Buglar—Sethe's sons; they run away from home in their teens

Ma'am—Sethe's unnamed mother.

Meanwhile, Back in the Story...

Sethe gets a job and moves in with Baby Suggs, who by this time has given up on God. She is ashamed of Him (and of herself) for the events leading to the baby's killing and she spends the rest of her life "pondering colors." Denver starts school, quits when a classmate asks about her mother, and is the first to hear a baby crawling on the stairs—though there is no baby. Mirrors break, furniture flies, baby fingerprints dent the butter. Sethe wonders if they should move to another house, but Baby Suggs says that every house in the country is haunted by *some dead Negro's grief.*

Howard, Sethe's eldest son, leaves home when the ghost begins shattering mirrors. Buglar holds on until tiny handprints appear in the frosting of a cake. Baby Suggs, worn out and oblivious to everything but color, barely notices the boys are gone; she dies like a run-down battery a few months after they leave. Sethe and Denver

try to entice the ghost to come out in the open, but it won't ... or can't.

"She wasn't even two years old when she died," Sethe said. "Too little to understand."

"Maybe she don't want to understand," said Denver.

"Maybe. But if only she'd come, I could make it clear to her."

The ghost tips tables, scoots sideboards, and does other spiteful things, but Sethe begins to feel that any sign of her beloved child is better than nothing. Denver, once she gets over her fright, realizes the little hell raiser is the only friend she has.

Which brings us back to the day the novel opens: Paul D thinks he is doing Sethe and Denver a favor by driving the ghost away, but Denver gets ornery when she realizes that he's chased away her only friend. Denver tries to make Paul feel unwelcome, but he's determined to win her over. There's a carnival in town with white performers; Paul, *"breathless with the excitement of seeing white people loose,"* takes Sethe and Denver to the carnival and spends his last two dollars on treats for them. On the walk home, they see a beautiful young woman sitting on a tree stump. She can't explain where she's come

from, she has a scar on her neck, she calls herself Beloved, and she's the same age Sethe's baby would have been if she'd lived. Denver recognizes her almost immediately, but Sethe doesn't have a clue. (Or is she repressing it?)

Paul and Sethe grow closer, as do Denver and Beloved. Paul, protective and suspicious, doesn't trust Beloved and wonders why Sethe lets her hang around. He questions Beloved about her past, but she says she has no idea who she is or where she came from. Denver, who could answer both questions, doesn't.

As Paul D and Sethe negotiate their way from a kind of sexy friendship toward love, tiny things become charged with significance. In an atmosphere where everyone's most passionate need is "beating back the past," Sethe's simple offer to let Paul "put his story next to hers" is so infused with love, courage, and respect that it almost hurts to read it. Paul D tells Sethe about being forced to wear a bit in his mouth like a horse and seeing a rooster that he swore was laughing at him because the rooster was freer than Paul.

For no exact reason, Paul moves out of Sethe's bed. They still make love, but he finds himself sleeping farther and farther away until he ends up in a cold storeroom. Through some power Paul can't understand, Beloved seduces him. He isn't seduced by her beauty so much as compelled by the intensity of—*what*?—her ravenous need to grab all the life she'd been deprived of? Her two-year-old mind in the body of a 20-year-old woman? Her need to exact a price from her mother? Her greedy love of her mother?

Paul didn't want it and didn't enjoy it, but he did it—so he tells Sethe he slept with Beloved and asks Sethe to have his child.

While she's thinking it over, a man named Stamp Paid (a well-meaning busybody in this situation, a sadly heroic figure in others) shows Paul a newspaper article about Sethe killing her child. Paul confronts Sethe, who explains that she was completely motivated by love. Paul, whose survival strategy is to love everything "just a little bit," tells Sethe that her love is "too thick." It's a discussion between people who disagree but care deeply for each other—until Paul D says, "You got two feet, Sethe, not four." That comes too close to Schoolteacher's lists of animal and human "characteristics" for Sethe to bear, and Paul D knew it as soon as he said it. He leaves; she's determined not to give a damn.

CHRONOLOGY (dates approximate)

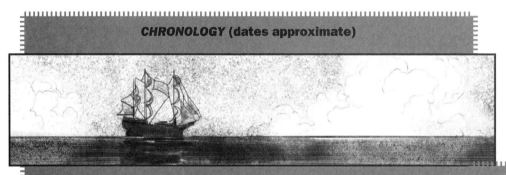

1518-
1850—Middle Passage: millions of Africans die in ships that take them across the Atlantic.

1795—Baby Suggs is born.

1838—The Garners buy Baby Suggs and Halle and bring them to Sweet Home.

1848—Sethe arrives at Sweet Home; Halle buys Baby Suggs' freedom.

1849-
1851—Sethe marries Halle; they have two sons; Baby Suggs lives in Cincinnati, free.

1853—Mr. Garner dies; Mrs. Garner sells Paul F.

1854—Beloved, Sethe and Halle's daughter, is born.

1855—Mrs. Garner sends for Schoolteacher; the slaves plan escape; pregnant Sethe sends her sons and Beloved to Baby Suggs; Schoolteacher's nephews suck Sethe's breast milk; Paul D, Halle, and Sixo try to escape; Sethe runs away; Sethe makes it to Baby Suggs' house; Schoolteacher tries to take her back to slavery; Sethe tries to kill her children and goes to jail; Sethe, released from jail, moves in with Baby Suggs.

Sethe can't bear the idea that anyone might feel sorry for her, so she takes Denver and Beloved ice skating on the frozen creek. They have a great time, laughing, tumbling across the ice. Back home, over a fire and warm milk, something clicks. Sethe realizes that Beloved is her dead baby and spends her savings on fancy clothes and food to appease the ghost. Driven by some combination of love and revenge, Beloved begins draining the life out of Sethe.

They run out of money, so Denver goes looking for work. A few of their neighbors give food and help, but by that time Beloved has nearly destroyed Sethe, and everyone knows it. Thirty women, townspeople who had avoided her like the plague for years, come to 124 to help Sethe get rid of Beloved. They join forces and sing the little monster out of Sethe's life! Meanwhile, Mr. Bodwin—an honorable old white guy who opposed slavery and owned 124 but had gone a bit senile in the last few years—comes riding up on a horse, wearing a black hat. Sethe, semi-cracked, but spiritually given a second chance, thinks Bodwin is the evil Schoolteacher and attacks him with an icepick. Denver and another woman stop her; Beloved seems to be gone for good, and Paul D wants to try making

1862-

1863—Denver (age 7) goes to school; a boy asks about Sethe's jail term; Denver quits school

1864—The ghost first appears; Denver hears it crawling on the stairs.

1865—Howard and Buglar leave home; Baby Suggs dies; the Civil War ends.

1873—August: The novel opens; Paul D turns up at 224; Paul, Sethe, and Denver go to the carnival and on the way home discover Beloved. Autumn: Paul moves out of Sethe's bed. Winter: Beloved seduces Paul, who he tells Sethe he slept with her.

1874—Stamp Paid shows Paul a clipping about Sethe killing her child ; Paul and Sethe split up.

1875—January: Sethe, Denver, and Beloved go skating; Sethe realizes that Beloved is her dead baby. April: Denver looks for work. Summer: Neighbors come to 124 to help Sethe get rid of Beloved.

a life with Sethe again. When Sethe is safe and subdued and they are sure that all is well, Paul D and Stamp Paid begin to laugh:

> *"Every time a whiteman come to the door she got to kill somebody?"*
> *"For all she know, the man could be coming for the rent."*
> *"Good thing they don't deliver mail out this way."*

That covers most of the factual events—but it barely touches the spiritual ones.

Toni Morrison Talks About *Beloved*

Elise Washington opens her 1987 interview with Toni Morrison for *Essence* magazine with this question: "If you were writing the book-jacket copy for *Beloved*, how would you describe it?"

"If I could understand it in a hundred words or less," TM replied, "I probably wouldn't have written the book."

What follows is a sampling of TM's remarks from the rest of that interview:

> *In hindsight, I think what's important about it is the process by which we construct and deconstruct reality in order to be able to function in it. I'm trying to explore how a people ... absorbs and rejects information on a very personal level about something [slavery] that is undigestible and unabsorbable....*
>
> *Those people had no value in the white world, so they made their own, and they decided what was valuable. It was usually something they were doing for somebody else. Nobody in the novel, no adult Black person, survives by self-regard, narcissism, selfishness.*
>
> *In some ways those were the most complicated of times, in some ways they were not. Now people choose their identities. Now people choose to be Black. They used to be born Black. That's not true anymore.*

And she had the following to say to Gail Caldwell:

> *What was on my mind was the way in which women are so vulnerable to displacing themselves, into something other than themselves.*

GAIL CALDWELL

The past, until you confront it, keeps coming back in other forms. The shapes redesign themselves in other constellations, until you get a chance to play it over again.

If you have trouble believing that an author can be the worst judge of her own work—and many people do—Morrison's reaction to *Beloved* novel was proof positive. She had originally conceived of the novel as a three-volume work, but, after writing for three years, became blocked and gave the partial manuscript to her editor, Bob Gottlieb, with apologies for her "failure."

"I had decided that I was never going to meet the deadline. I gave Bob what I had, and said, 'I'm sorry, because I have only a third of a book.'

"And he read it and said, 'Whatever else you're doing, do it, but this is a book.' I said, 'Are you sure?'"

Morrison couldn't believe it and asked Gottlieb again if he was sure. He was. Except for a page-and-a-half coda at the end, she had given him *Beloved*.

What Did the Critics Say?

Beloved got spectacular reviews—

[In this] magnificent novel ... [a slave's] interior life is re-created with a moving intensity no novelist has even approached before. The splintered, piecemeal revelation of the past is one of the technical wonders of Morrison's narrative.... I think we have a masterpiece on our hands here: difficult, sometimes lushly overwritten, but profoundly imagined and carried out with burning fervor.

–Walter Clemons, *Newsweek*

Ms. Morrison's versatility and technical and emotional range appear to know no bounds. Beloved is rich, graceful, eccentric, rough, lyrical, sinuous, colloquial and very much to the point. In this book, the other world exists and magic works, and the prose is up to it. If you can believe page one—and Ms. Morrison's verbal authority compels belief—you're hooked on the rest of the book.

–Margaret Atwood, *The New York Times Book Review*

JOHN LEONARD

From Them (Through Her) to Us

Beloved is generally considered Toni Morrison's most difficult book, but in some ways it's the most straightforward. You can't read it without knowing that it's "about" slavery as a personal experience. And you can't miss the fact that it's an intimate, incredibly personal novel from her to us. Or, from *them*, through her, to us. The feeling you get is that Morrison could not have written *Beloved*—nobody

could have—she must have *channeled* it. It's easy to imagine that the slaves themselves whispered it in her ear. (In a way, of course, they did.)

Aside from the raw experience of slavery, *Beloved* is about love—above all, the unbounded love of a mother for her children. And Morrison is talking to all of us, of course, offering an opportunity to transcend gender, geography, and time. The novel allows us to become Sethe, a strong and resourceful woman who loves her children so much that she is willing to risk anything, including the wrath of God, to save them from slavery. She manages to "save" only one of her children before she is restrained. She rejects the censure of her neighbors and refuses to feel guilt before God. There is only one person in the world she is answerable to. You are Sethe. The child you killed out of love wants to have a word with you...

Beloved is about all of that and more. But when you read it, be prepared. No doubt you'll ask yourself over and over again, *How could she do it? And how could Morrison have endured the pain to write it?*

The way the characters survive it is the way most people survive the truly unbearable events of their lives: by repressing it. Everyone in the novel believes that the way to freedom lies in forgetting the past. Baby Suggs, a character so glorious—a *person* so glorious—that her spiritual exhaustion is almost as shattering as Sethe's killing of her child, goes so far as to forbid any talk of slavery. And if, in fact, survival does depend on forgetting, then they're all doomed, because the past keeps leaking in. Through all the voices and memories, including those of Sethe's mother, a survivor of the Middle Passage, we get a taste of slavery from the viewpoint of its victims.

As novelist Margaret Atwood put it, "Above all, it [slavery] is seen as one of the most viciously anti-family institutions human beings have ever devised." The life experience of Baby Suggs makes the point in starker terms:

> **Anybody Baby Suggs knew, let alone loved, who hadn't been run off or been hanged, got rented out, loaned out, bought up, brought back ... mortgaged, won, stolen or seized.**

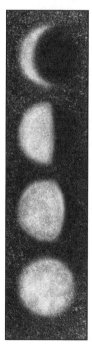

Seeing it Whole

It takes a bit of work to uncover the structure of a novel, but when the book's rhythm feels as elegant as *Beloved*'s, it's exciting to discover how it got that way and to see what surprises it reveals.

Toni Morrison typically selects an image to help her "see" her novel as she writes it. To look at it and SEE the novel as if it were a painting or a piece of sculpture. To take in its shape, structure, and design—its *architecture*.

In the case of *Beloved*, you *can* see the relationship of each Part to the Whole. Several things are immediately apparent: Part One is nearly twice as long as Parts Two and Three combined. The total number of chapters (28) corresponds to the lunar/menstrual cycle. (Hey, it's a book about women.)

Each of the three Parts begins with a long chapter that describes the state of the house (124) as it goes from "*spiteful*" to "*loud*" to "*quiet*." Many of the chapters are very short for a Morrison novel, just two to seven pages).

And feel the surprising rhythm of WHEN things happen:

Beloved, the title character, doesn't appear until Chapter 5.

Sethe doesn't fully realize that Beloved is her daughter until Chapter 19, two-thirds of the way into the book.

The four chapters shaded in the table that follows are the only difficult parts of the book, but notice where they're placed (after page 200) and how brief they are.

If you have already read the novel, you may have noticed that the language in Part One is much

IN THIS MOMENT...

more restrained than we've come to expect from Toni Morrison. Toward the end of Part One, as we near the climactic scene, the language gets more expansive. By the time TM gets to the four Stream-of-Consciousness chapters in Part Two (shaded in gray), she knows she can dynamite the language without scaring off less experienced readers. Even then, she doesn't test your patience by making the sections long. These four chapters (20–23) are what writers call Streams of Consciousness or Interior Monologues— attempts to reproduce the thought process itself, as if you spoke your uncensored thoughts into a tape-recorder.

Ch.20: ("Beloved, she my daughter."): Sethe's stream-of-consciousness

Ch.21: ("Beloved is my sister."): Denver's stream-of-consciousness

Ch.22: ("I am Beloved and she is mine. I see..."): Beloved's "Middle Passage" stream-of-consciousness

Ch.23: ("I am Beloved and she is mine. Sethe..."): Beloved's stream-of-consciousness and poetic dialogue

PART ONE

PART TWO

PART THREE

*P = page number on which chapter begins

**L = length of chapter

(Plume paperback edition)

The Stream of Consciousness Chapters (more detail)

Chapter 20: *Beloved, she my daughter.*

Sethe ruminates on being a mother and on her own mother, Ma'am, who survived the Middle Passage and was forced to nurse white children. Sethe's mind wanders through the past, telling Mrs. Garner that the nephews violated her breasts; Mrs. Garner, a helpless invalid, couldn't do anything about it. Sethe, above all, is obsessed with Beloved.

Chapter 21: *Beloved is my sister.*
Denver recollects her brothers' fears that their mother might kill them like she killed Beloved. Denver admits she's a recluse, always on the alert that her mother might kill her, too. Her mission is to protect Beloved from their mother.

Chapter 22: *I am Beloved and she is mine. I see...*
Beloved's "Middle Passage" stream-of-consciousness, this is by far the most difficult chapter—sentences without punctuation and phrases that seem to be elbowing each other out of the way. But try to relax and don't exactly read it. Treat it as if it were a piece of music, NOT intended to transmit "word" information but to evoke a mood, give voice, pay homage, and honor the millions of Africans killed during the Middle Passage. In death, Beloved merged with her own dead ancestors in an underwater nightmare of the Collective Unconscious. One reason it isn't easy reading is that, to TM's credit, she wouldn't take the easy way and let Beloved have a grown-up mind even for a few pages. She was a two-year-old child at the bottom of the ocean. Beloved, despite having her body cast into the ocean and her soul left to wander among those of dead ancestors, longs for life and her mother: "she is my face smiling at me".

Chapter 23: *I am Beloved and she is mine. Sethe...*
Beloved's stream-of-consciousness and poetic dialogue, easier than the preceding one. Then it turns into a kind of poetic dialogue between Sethe and Beloved, then Denver and Beloved, then all three, in which they all seem to want to possess each other. The trio of voices ends as many curses, incantations, and prayers end—repeated three times: *You are mine. You are mine. You are mine.*

SYMBOLS AND MOTIFS IN *BELOVED*

milk = motherhood

water = divides earth from afterlife

river = divides freedom and slavery

124 [the House Number] is repeated like a motif or mantra; 1+2+4 = 7, a key number in religion and myth

red = Beloved's signature color; as a spirit "a pool of red undulating light"

colors = the inability to see them signifies a closing-off of the senses and withdrawal of the self

corn = female genitalia ("how loose the silk")

fingers and hands = healing, comforting

breastfeeding = comforting, caring

Sweet Home = both Eden and Hell; parody of "My Old Kentucky Home"

shadows = hidden truths

Baby Suggs = Earth Mother, nurturer

unlined hands = signifies a ghost

Sethe's lack of bladder control (when she sees Beloved) = before a woman gives birth, her "water breaks"

Sethe's "diamonds" = crystal earrings, a wedding present from Mrs. Garner

heart = nurturing, the "prize"

way station = a safe place for runaway slaves [or wandering spirits]

Paul D's journey = Odysseus' journey [Homer's Greek epic, *The Odyssey*]

tobacco tin = metaphor for where Paul D kept bad memories; the lid flies off when he has sex with Beloved

Four Horsemen = schoolteacher, one nephew, a slave catcher, and a sheriff; the Four Horsemen of the Apocalypse: famine, war, pestilence and death

"the men without skin" = white men

The narrative structure of *Beloved* is downright beautiful. In **Chapter 8**, there is a seamless transition from Denver and Beloved telling a story to the story actually happening. In **Chapter 9**, there is an elegant transition from Ella's point of view to Sethe's. In **Chapter 16**, TM shifts the point of view, stunningly, to the white slave catchers. Again and again, consciousness is passed from person to person like a baton in a relay race. The narrative structure is complex and subtle, but you can feel the logic in the shifts. The language is powerful without overwhelming the characters. It is as if there is no author, no ego, no anything between the people in the book and us (though this changes somewhat toward the end.)

More than any of her other works, *Beloved* holds together as a Eurocentric novel. TM doesn't swerve off track into beautiful but irrelevant digressions. She doesn't people *Beloved* with fascinating characters the novel doesn't need. Her earlier novels often seemed to be made of pieces that could be moved, removed, or shifted from book to book without greatly changing the character. (TM herself described *The Bluest Eye* and *Sula* as "pieces of a broken mirror.") But in *Beloved*, everything connects, everything fits—each of the parts contributes to the whole. The chain of causality is always convincing, and the suspense never seems forced or artificially prolonged.

At last count, Toni Morrison had actualized all but two of the 11 qualities she had prioritized for the African American novel:

- **an obligation to bear witness**
- **a novel that would take her people through the pain and denial of their racially haunted history to a healing zone**

The amazing thing is that *Beloved* was designed consciously and intentionally to achieve these two goals, but the novel itself doesn't feel stiff or artificial or manipulative in any way. It feels like it was born, not written!

All that said, let us end this chapter with some of the most life-affirming wordmusic ever written. Baby Suggs, Sethe's old and gimpy mother-in-law, wonders at first why her son had worked his brains out to buy her freedom. She couldn't imagine what good it could be or what she was going to do with it ... until she experiences it.

And when she does experience it, she becomes Holy. She gathers her people in the field and says things that make them, and us, Holy:

> **She did not tell them to clean up their lives or to go and sin no more. She did not tell them they were the blessed of the earth, its inheriting meek or its glorybound pure.**
> **She told them that the only grace they could have was the grace they could imagine. That if they could not see it, they would not have it.**

The prayer goes on for a few hundred more words. Read it to the end, and consider re-reading it to yourself every day.

In May 2006, the editors of *The New York Times Book Review* sent a letter to several hundred writers, critics, and other notable literary figures, asking them to name "the single best work of American fiction published in the last 25 years." The solid winner was *Beloved*.

Amen to that.

Jazz was my attempt to reclaim the era from F. Scott Fitzgerald. But it also uses the techniques of jazz—improvisation, listening—to ask questions that I want to ask of myself.

–Toni Morrison, "The Art of Teaching,"
Interview with Ann Hostetler, 2002

JAZZ
(1992)

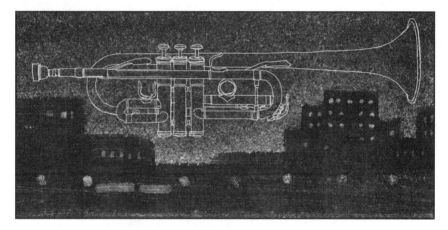

When Toni Morrison first conceived *Beloved,* she thought of it as the first part of a trilogy—a novel with three independent sections, set in three different times. The second part was to be set in 1920s Harlem, but Morrison had trouble finishing it and—as you'll recall from the last chapter—gave the "unfinished" manuscript to editor Bob Gottlieb with apologies for her "failure." Gottlieb, quickly realizing it was a masterpiece, published it as *Beloved* and sent TM home to await the Pulitzer Prize and other acclaim.

Among other things, this meant that Morrison had to face a new reality about her work: What she had thought of as a middle—the book about Harlem in the 1920s—was actually a beginning.

As in the case of *Beloved,* the idea came from something she had read. Several years earlier, she had seen a book by photographer

James Van Der Zee titled *The Harlem Book of the Dead,* a collection of photos taken in the 1920s of dead black New Yorkers. It was the fashion of the day to dress your deceased loved ones in their fanciest threads and take pictures of them lying elegantly in their coffins or being cradled lovingly in your arms. Morrison was especially intrigued by the picture of a 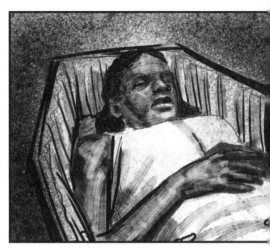 dead girl lying in a coffin. The accompanying text explained that she was 18 years old and had been dancing at a "rent party" when she suddenly slumped over. Friends rushed to help, saw blood streaming out of her, and realized that she must have been shot.

"What happened?" her friends asked.

The girl knew that her jealous ex-boyfriend had shot her, but she still loved him and wanted him to get away. So she said to her friends, "I'll tell you tomorrow." And she died.

Historical Background

In 1918, with the end of the "the war to end all wars," the spirit of rebirth that energized much of the world held even greater promise for black Americans. At the turn of the twentieth century, lack of economic opportunity had rendered Emancipation a sick joke. As of 1900, 75% of America's black population still lived in the South, working on cotton plantations as "wage slaves" rather than literal slaves. After the Great War, however, factories opening in northern cities offered real jobs. Blacks by the thousands migrated to cities like Detroit, Chicago, and New York, triggering a time of great vitality in African American life. Black music and dance expressed the national mood in the 1920s and gave it a nickname—the Jazz Age.

Harlem, New York City, the intellectual and artistic center of this black awakening, experienced a collective rebirth that became known as the Harlem Renaissance. Throughout the 1920s, black poetry, art, dance, literature, and other expressions of repressed black genius burst into full bloom. Jazz, an authentic African American art form, was the jewel.

There might not have been any jazz in Harlem if it weren't for Southerners. In the early 1920s, most Northerners thought of jazz as Paul Whiteman's and George Gershwin's watered-down white versions. So when black musicians from the South—virtually all of jazz's early masters were Southern—brought real jazz and "pre-jazz" (blues, ragtime, stride, etc.) to Harlem, it was like putting one of those electric zappers to a half-dead man's heart. In an instant, jazz became the heartbeat of the Harlem Renaissance. Throughout the 1920s, jazz lovers of all colors flocked to Harlem to hear Duke Ellington, Fletcher Henderson, Bessie Smith, Louis Armstrong, and other great artists in flashy night spots like the Cotton Club. In residential areas, locals held "rent parties," hiring musicians to play in their apartments and charging a small fee to cover the week's rent. As often as not, these thrown-together little rent parties featured great jazz pianists like Fats Waller and James P. Johnson. These musicians weren't just playing jazz—they were inventing it.

But what about the "regular people," the thousands of southern blacks who had moved north in search of a better life ... the ones who had no idea they were living through something fancy called the Harlem Renaissance? *Jazz* is their story.

The Story

Toni Morrison's sixth novel, *Jazz* ends on the very first page:

> *Sth, I know that woman. She used to live with a flock of birds on Lenox Avenue. Know her husband, too. He fell for an eighteen-year-old girl with one of those deepdown, spooky loves that made him*

so sad and happy he shot her just to keep the feeling going. When the woman, her name is Violet, went to the funeral to see the girl and to cut her dead face they threw her to the floor and out of the church.

This paragraph raises a number of questions (though its gossipy beauty sets the tone of the novel so sweetly that you might want to read it again before we ask them):

Why did a mature married man fall for an 18-year-old girl? Was it because of something lacking in his wife or because of something lacking in himself—or was he just another old lech sniffing after some young hips? Why didn't he settle for a roll in the sack instead of falling in "deepdown, spooky love"? Why shoot the girl? Why does his wife Violet crash the funeral? Why does she try to disfigure the girl's face *after* she's dead? Was Violet a stable person who temporarily lost it because of her husband's affair ... or was she a little whacked out to begin with? How do the man and wife react after the funeral? How do they cope? (Or do they?) And the young girl's family, friends, neighbors—how do they feel about the killer and his wife? And this 18 year-old girl—what was special about her?

Finally, who's telling us the story? ("Sth" isn't even a name or word.)

Jazz, the story of Joe and Violet Trace, is a dark ballad of love, murder, and coming to terms with your actions when they're out of whack with the rest of your life. Born, raised, and married in the South, Joe and Violet had come to Harlem so full of hope that even the train ride from Virginia felt like dancing. Twenty years later, their world had shrunk and nothing, including dancing, felt like dancing. Violet was a hairdresser who fell through the cracks and gave the meager remains of her affection to her birds. Joe was a 50-year-old door-to-door cosmetics salesman who remembered the conduct of love but couldn't quite "catch what it felt like."

The year is 1926, smack in the middle of Harlem's cultural explosion. Three hundred years of unsung love songs and uncelebrated funerals came screaming out in every imaginable form, from poetry and painting to philosophy and fashion. Above all, music: jazz in particular. The music, the city streets, the vibe in the air create an "appetite," a communal longing. DO IT!—whatever it is. Joe Trace meets Dorcas Manfred, a teenager whose parents had been killed in the 1919 East St. Louis race riots. He falls crazy in love.

As is typically the case in a Toni Morrison novel, the story unfolds, chunk by chunk, toward both future and past. We get a few pages about Violet after the funeral and a few pages about her recent past. Violet had been acting funny for the last year or so; Joe could see that, but he could also see that she kept it together in public. So as far as Joe was concerned, she was fine. What neither Violet nor the neighbors had noticed was that she'd recently had a couple "episodes" in public. Before we get too worried, however, TM gives us a couple nice pages about Joe and Dorcas both before and after the murder, then Joe further back in time. We hear about friends and family, New York and Down South. We learn about Joe's and Violet's background. We learn that Dorcas was neither pretty nor interesting and that Joe is more interesting than he first seemed (a natural woodsman who reinvents himself every few years). We learn that Violet's mother committed suicide because she couldn't bear the pressure of supporting her children (her grandmother raised her) and that Violet was a strong and assertive young woman until recently, when she began leaking through the cracks.

We meet Alice Manfred, Dorcas' aunt, a strong, responsible woman who raised Dorcas too strictly so as to protect her from the big city and that "dirty, get-on-down music." Not that Dorcas needed much encouraging. She was a shallow, self-absorbed 18-year-old, obsessed with her looks, clothing, and sex—not a character Morrison had made especially sympathetic. (It's interesting to remember that Dorcas might have been the 1920s version of Beloved.)

THE MAJOR CHARACTERS

Narrators—Seemingly several, all unnamed, implied people or objects—all unreliable...

Violet Trace—The main character. She's a hairdresser, married to Joe Trace for 20 years. On the verge of losing her husband and her sanity. When her husband shoots his lover, Violet tries to disfigure the corpse's face.

Joe Trace—The "other" main character, Violet's husband, a cosmetics salesman, around 50 years-old.

Dorcas Manfred—The girl Joe falls in love with, then kills. She's 18 years old, her parents were killed, she's being raised by her aunt Alice. Her main interest is exploring her sexuality.

Alice Manfred—Dorcas' aunt (her mom's sister), fairly well-off; a strict "parent."

Wild—Joe Trace's mother.

Golden Gray—Joe's father, half-black but white-skinned. When he finds out his father is black, he vows to kill him.

Rose Dear—Violet's mother. Overwhelmed by the pressure of trying to support her children, she commits suicide.

True Belle—Violet's grandmother, Rose Dear's mother; she takes care of the family after Rose Dear commits suicide

Violet's father (unnamed)—He drops by once in a while, gives everyone a gift, then splits. He's never around when you need him.

Malvonne—Joe and Violet's upstairs neighbor. She lets Joe and Dorcas meet secretly in her apartment (but feels guilty about it).

Sweetness—Malvonne's shifty nephew (he steals people's mail looking for money).

Acton—Dorcas' new young boyfriend.

Felice—Dorcas' best friend, raised by her grandmother, becomes friends with Joe and Violet.

Oddly enough, it's the men in Morrison's novels who are usually the doomed romantics. Dorcas urges Joe to leave her, but Joe won't (or can't). When Dorcas takes up with Acton, a young man around her own age, Joe goes looking for her. Like the hunter he was Down South, he spends five days tracing her movements. After he tracks her to a crowded apartment and finds her dancing with her young man, Joe doesn't exactly realize that he's shot her. When he hears the gun go off, he wants to "catch her before she fell and hurt herself."

Violet's description of her own behavior at the funeral, where she tried to slash Dorcas' face, is even more disassociated: she watched as "a woman she recognized" elbowed her way through the mourners and raised a knife over the dead girl's face. Later, Violet tells Alice Manfred how silly she must have looked busting into Dorcas' funeral, fumbling with the knife, "trying to do something bluesy"—and both women burst into healing laughter.

The scenes between Violet and Alice are some of the best in the book. Alice doesn't want anything to do with the lunatic wife of the man who killed her niece. Violet wants to learn more about Dorcas so she can hate the girl more precisely, but Violet finds herself beginning to like Dorcas, even thinking of her as the daughter she might have had; Alice realizes how much she and Violet have in common.

When Dorcas' best friend Felice enters the story, we expect all hell to break loose. The narrator says that she (or he or it) is certain that either Joe or Violet would "kill the other." But nobody kills anybody. Felice had come to tell Joe what really happened with Dorcas to absolve him of his guilt and to tell him to stop grieving because she wasn't worth it. Dorcas had only been wounded in the shoulder and could have easily saved herself, according to Felice, but she was too lazy to go to the hospital or to let anyone take her. She insisted on going to sleep and bled to death unnecessarily. Felice had planned to just tell the story and leave, but she liked Joe and Violet so much that she told them about herself and her "unusual" friendship with Dorcas. It was unusual because Dorcas was light-skinned and Felice was very dark. (Even inside the black community, people often "segregated" themselves by color.)

Before Dorcas died, she'd asked Felice to tell Joe about "the apple," referencing a story she and Joe shared. The implication was that Dorcas not only forgave Joe, but considered him her first love. By the time Felice leaves Joe and Violet, it's clear that the three of them have become a family. The book ends with all the right people being happy in a modest way.

Except for the Narrator! The Narrator is upset about jumping to the wrong conclusion in thinking that Felice would be like Dorcas and Joe or Violet would be killed.

HENRY LOUIS GATES, JR

Did the Critics Love *Jazz*?

In contrast to the overwhelming critical acclaim for *Beloved*, the response to *Jazz* was lukewarm. The book got some decent reviews, even a couple of great ones. John Leonard, in a long, breathless rumination on TM's career, said what he always said: Toni Morrison is "the best writer working in America." Edna O'Brien, the fine Irish novelist, offered some praise for *Jazz* but felt that the characters never came to life. TM, she said, had become "bedazzled by her own virtuosity."

One of the more interesting takes on the novel came from African American scholar Henry Louis Gates, Jr.:

Others disagreed, pointing out that modernist writers like Faulkner, James Joyce, and Virginia Woolf had used similar techniques more than 50 earlier without invoking jazz aesthetics.

Was that her purpose anyway? If so, how successful was she? What jazz techniques did she use and what were their plausible explanations?

Mirroring the Music ... or NOT?

Q: Did Toni Morrison intend to make *Jazz* (the novel) a literary representation of jazz (the music)?

A: Yes. In her own words: "[T]he jazz-like structure wasn't a secondary thing for me—it was the raison d'etre of the book. The process of trial and error by which the narrator revealed the plot was as important and exciting to me as telling the story." (*Paris Review*, Fall 1993) Morrison's novel is not *about* jazz, it aspires to *be* jazz.

> [H]er hand, the one that wasn't holding the glass shaped like a flower, was under the table drumming out the rhythm on the inside of his thigh, his thigh, thigh, thigh....

Q: In what ways does her writing mirror the music?

A: TM began with the idea of a jazz trio, the most basic jazz group. In *Jazz*, the basic trio is comprised of Joe Trace, Violet Trace, and Dorcas, Joe's young lover. The trio would play a melody, then take turns improvising on it.

Q: Are there any other ways?

A: Yes. She wanted her book to reconcile the (almost) mutually exclusive goals of being both improvised and composed. Jazz music is generally made up of ... theme, solo, solo, solo, theme. Call and Response. Improvisations—above all, improvisations. Each player (or reader) improvises on—and transforms—the theme. Loving Dorcas, then killing her, is Joe's solo. Disfiguring Dorcas is Violet's solo. (Violet said it was her attempt to do "something bluesy.")

As for Call and Response, Morrison uses it in a variety of ways in *Jazz*, from the unsubtle echoes of Violet's parrot ("I love you") to the series of gentle introductions at the start of each new Part of the novel.

And finally—amazingly—Morrison imports not only the music of jazz, but the *performance* of jazz as well. Here's how: In any live performance, there will be mistakes. At its best, live jazz takes those mistakes and uses them to move the music in a direction that surprises everyone. Morrison (her genius is astonishing!) parallels this technique in her novel by having the book's Narrators make mistakes. The Narrators in *Jazz* actually admit they've made mistakes, whereupon the book zooms off in another direction! The radical art of mirroring in-performance "mistakes" and turning them into new behaviors is one of TM's most elegant stylistic achievements in this novel.

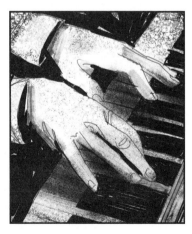

Looking For Structure...

Jazz is divided into ten parts that are clearly intentional, but a bit mystifying. Start with what you know: TM begins each section of *Jazz* by connecting the beginning of a chapter to the end of the preceding chapter. Either it echoes the previous passage or answers its questions or elaborates on it ... whatever. A couple of examples:

Chapter 1 ends with: *"I love you."*

Chapter 2 begins with: *Or used to.*

Chapter 3 ends with: *...a woman sitting by her ironing board in a hat in the morning.*

Chapter 4 begins with: *The hat, pushed back on her forehead, gave Violet a scatty look.*

TM provides a gentle intro to each new section by opening chapters with a "riff" (either *repetition* with some minor changes or *elaboration*) on the ending of the previous chapter. In doing so, TM adopts a subtle version of the Call-and-Response theme that has been part of African music for centuries. In *Jazz*, the responses are not mere continuations of the story. More often than not they involve different characters and different situations. The words are passed from one soloist to another.

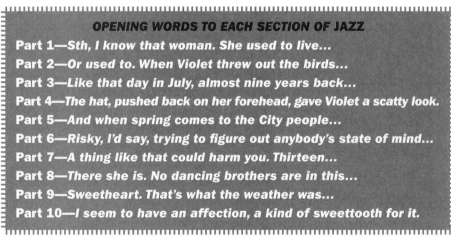

OPENING WORDS TO EACH SECTION OF JAZZ

Part 1—*Sth, I know that woman. She used to live...*
Part 2—*Or used to. When Violet threw out the birds...*
Part 3—*Like that day in July, almost nine years back...*
Part 4—*The hat, pushed back on her forehead, gave Violet a scatty look.*
Part 5—*And when spring comes to the City people...*
Part 6—*Risky, I'd say, trying to figure out anybody's state of mind...*
Part 7—*A thing like that could harm you. Thirteen...*
Part 8—*There she is. No dancing brothers are in this...*
Part 9—*Sweetheart. That's what the weather was...*
Part 10—*I seem to have an affection, a kind of sweettooth for it.*

In a jazz group, each soloist gets a chance to improvise on the basic melody. Morrison has described her idealized version of jazz improvisation in terms of the great jazz pianist Keith Jarrett playing "Ol' Man River." The thrill for a listener, TM says, doesn't come when Jarrett (or she) plays the original melody; the thrill comes when the listener or reader recognizes bits of the original melody after it's been fragmented and hidden by the improvisation.

The Narrator

In most novels, the narrator isn't an issue. In *Jazz*, it most certainly is...

Q: Who is telling this story? Is it one person (or THING)—or several of them?

A: Several.

Q: Is it my imagination or does or does the Narrator change his, her, or its mind?

A: It is not your imagination.

Q: What's up with that chaos of Quotation Marks? Me or "Me"—What the hell is the difference?

A: Tricky question, but it may be that the quote marks are meant to differentiate between the fallible "human" Narrator and the "omniscient" (all-knowing) Narrator. For example, if the story is being told from the point of view of Joe Trace the Human Being, the "monologue" is set in quotation marks (as if Joe himself were talking to you). But if Joe's story is told *without* quotation marks, here the Omniscient Narrator is telling us about Joe Trace. So the purpose of that tortuous mess of quotation marks might be to signify the difference between Joe's (or whomever's) version of the truth and the real, Objective Truth. All of this is further complicated by the fact that the Omniscient Narrators don't necessarily agree with one another and that there are a host of other bizarre Narrators, including Toni Morrison, inanimate objects (like the book itself!), and maybe even God. All of them, including God and Toni Morrison, are what writers classify as "Unreliable Narrators."

Q: Why would Toni Morrison do something so preposterously complex?

A: Because, she says, she wants to draw attention to the point that American literature is too "totalized"—that is, everything is presented from one point of view. She's right, of course, but her version of the cure feels worse than the disease!

Q: Be that as it may, ladies and gentlemen of the jury, have you reached a final verdict?

A: Yes, your Honor.

Q: Will you read your verdict to the court, please?

A: We find the defendant guilty of Virtuosity in the First Degree.

By way of further evidence—the last two paragraphs of the book:

> I envy them [Joe and Violet] *their public love. I myself have only known it in secret, shared it in secret and longed, aw longed to show it—to be able to say out loud what they have no need to say at all: That I have loved only you, surrendered my whole self reckless to you and nobody else. That I want you to love me back and show it to me. That I love the way you hold me, how close you let me be to you. I like your fingers on and on, lifting, turning. I have watched your face for a long time now, and missed your eyes when you went away from me. Talking to you and hearing you answer—that's the kick.*
>
> *But I can't say that aloud; I can't tell anyone that I have been waiting for this all my life and that being chosen to wait is the reason I can. If I were able I'd say it. Say make me, remake me. You are free to do it and I am free to let you because look, look. Look where your hands are. Now.*

Reading that passage, it's hard not to feel like Robert De Niro in *Taxi Driver,* staring into the mirror...

You talkin' to ME?

You talkin' about MY hands? MY fingers? MY face?

"I am the whore, and the holy one. I am the wife and the virgin. I am [the mother] and the daughter...."
—"Thunder, Perfect Mind," *Nag Hammadi*

PARADISE
(1997)

Paradise is one of the strangest, most devious, most brilliant books you'll ever read. No reviews convey the actual *experience* of reading it.

The novel begins with this grim announcement:

> **They shoot the white girl first. With the rest they can take their time.**

Although reviewers have offered confident but differing opinions as to who the white girl is, even by the end of the book, *nobody* is sure.

The second paragraph:

> **They are nine, over twice the number of the women they are obliged to stampede or kill and they have the paraphernalia for either requirement: rope, a palm leaf cross, handcuffs, Mace and sunglasses, along with clean, handsome guns.**

Anyone who reads *Paradise* knows that FIVE women are killed, but nobody has seen fit to mention that the "nine" men mentioned again and again are NOT *"over twice the number of women"* they set out to kill. (That would be at least 11.)

Nor does any critic notice something profoundly idiotic about killers whose arsenal includes a palm leaf cross and sunglasses!

And nobody mentions the fact that Deek and Steward Morgan, who remember "everything that ever happened," recall that *"one hundred and fifty-eight"* of their ancestors left but later say *"all seventy-nine were lost."* (Note that 158 is exactly double 79!)

Early in the novel, the attackers discover a gum wrapper. Doublemint gum. Six lines later, we learn that the leaders of the attack are twins. One minute you think you're reading a strangle-slaughter-mangle novel, the next minute up pop the Doublemint Twins!

Has Toni Morrison, one of the most serious women in the universe, turned into a gag writer?

A Bit of Background

After finishing *Jazz* (1992), TM settled on an obscure bit of American history for her next novel. When the Civil War was over, groups of former slaves headed into Oklahoma and other sparsely populated Western states to set up all-black towns in the wide-open spaces we usually associate with cowboys.

Morrison, on a research trip to Brazil, heard about a convent run by black nuns who took in abandoned children and, as TM put it, "practiced Catholicism on the first floor and *candomblé* in the basement." (*Candomblé* is the Brazilian version of voodoo—both of which are folk religions, not witchcraft.) According to one version of the story, a posse of local men went on a rampage and killed the nuns.

And the ex-slaves in Oklahoma? Two things in particular grabbed Morrison's attention: several newspaper ads inviting black people to join the new communities contained the enigmatic warning, "Come Prepared or Not at All"; and at least one of the black communities had an unusual way of organizing their town—their Paradise—in terms of color.

The novel opens with the two brutal paragraphs quoted above and continues along similar lines—stalking, shooting, kicking, and blaming with the utter calm and peace that passeth all understanding that only men who think they are doing God's work can hide behind. After a full chapter of *that*, the men corner the women:

> **"God at their side, the men take aim. For Ruby."**

Paradise: The Surface

Paradise is essentially two separate books that overlap occasionally and finally meet, tragically, at the end. One book is the story of the all-black town of Ruby, Oklahoma—its citizens, its founders, its reason for being, and its difficulties in trying to maintain its identity. The other book is the story of a place called the Convent and the five women who meet and die there.

The slaughter that frames the book is set in Oklahoma in 1976. The rest takes place between 1968 and 1976, with flashbacks going back to 1870. The novel is divided into nine sections, each named for a woman. The opening section, like their beloved town, is called Ruby, after Deacon and Steward Morgan's deceased sister. Although Ruby has a population of only 360, the novel that tells its story seems to have more characters than the Bible. In order to understand Ruby, Oklahoma (founded 1950), it is important to understand its predecessor, Haven, Oklahoma Territory (founded 1890).

The Disallowing

During the 1880s, a group of ex-slaves from Louisiana and Mississippi, led by nine patriarchs, traveled west to settle in the

Oklahoma Territory. After much difficulty, they reached the all-black town of Fairly and asked its leaders if they could stay. The people of Fairly said *No*. Why? The citizens of Fairly were light-skinned blacks, and the newcomers were dark-skinned. *Very* dark. They called themselves "8-Rocks"—men with skin the color of coal from deep in the mines. That rejection, which the outcasts called the Disallowing, became the defining event in their lives.

The outcasts eventually built their own town, which they called Haven.

Haven and Ruby

Haven was established in 1890, the same year they built the communal Oven, a symbol of their isolation. Haven thrived until the mid-1930s, when young folks began leaving. With the start of World War II, more young men, including the Morgan twins—Deacon and Steward—joined the Army. When they returned to Haven after the war, no one seemed to care if they were home or not. So Deek, Steward, their sister Ruby, and 14 other families dismantled the Oven and headed west to find a new home. The place they settled was in the middle of nowhere. They named it Ruby, in honor of the twins' sister who died after the journey.

The only place within 90 miles was an old house called the Convent.

The Convent

The Convent had started out as an embezzler's mansion, with statues of naked ladies, doorknobs with nipples, and phallic water faucets. After the embezzler was spirited off to jail, the place was taken over by nuns and turned into a school for Native American girls. The nuns got rid of some of the porn fixtures and ignored the rest. By the time Mavis (the first of the four drop-in "guests" that die in the slaughter) arrives at the Convent in 1968, only two people remain: the old, bed-ridden Mother Superior and Connie, the woman who cares for her.

The backgrounds of the characters appear in bits and pieces throughout the novel. Although each of the nine sections is named for a female character, the sections are not devoted entirely to the title character.

Mavis

The second section, titled Mavis, begins in Maryland in 1968 as Mavis is being interviewed by a journalist because her newborn twins had suffocated in the back seat of her Cadillac. Mavis is stupid and pathetic, but she loves her husband's Cadillac. So she steals the car and, after a visit with her mother, heads toward  California. Airhead that she is, she runs out of gas a couple miles from the Convent. Instead of waiting for help, as she usually does, Mavis walks to the Convent.

Grace

The next chapter, Grace, takes the name of a sex-bomb who calls herself Gigi and gets off the bus in Ruby a few years after Mavis. Gigi is such a tootsieroll that the mere sight of her crossing the street stuns the sidewalk studs into silence. K.D. Morgan, the twins' useless nephew, strolls by with his pregnant girlfriend, Arnette. Arnette doesn't take kindly to K.D. gaping at the big-boobed stranger and calls her a "tramp." K.D. slaps her, which occasions a town meeting.

We get a taste of the Morgan twins 20 years after the founding of Ruby. They are the wealthiest and smartest brothers in town, but they have a problem: Steward and his wife Dovey can't have children, and Deek and his wife Soane's two sons both were killed in Vietnam. There is no one to carry on the family line.

At the meeting between the families, we meet the new preacher, Reverend Misner, a defender—or instigator—of the young. We also meet Arnette's brother Jeff, whose free-floating desire to kill someone is only slightly more urgent than Steward Morgan's.

Seneca

The fourth section introduces Seneca, a painfully timid 20-year-old. After her abusive boyfriend Eddie is sent to jail, Seneca hitchhikes to Wichita to see Eddie's mother. Seneca is too shy to hitchhike out of Wichita, so she stows away in parked trucks and ends up wherever they stop. When she sees Jeff Fleetwood's crazy wife Sweetie crying along the road, Seneca jumps out of the truck to comfort her; she and Sweetie wander into the Convent.

The Fight Over the Oven

The tension between the youngsters of Ruby and their elders had been brewing for months. The Oven was the symbolic center of the community, so when the kids demand the right to change its inscription from "Beware the Furrow of His Brow" to "BE the Furrow of His Brow," all hell breaks loose. The fire-breathing Reverend Pulliam flips out. *Beware the Furrow of His Brow,* he says,

is *"not a suggestion, it is an order."* The kids don't want to take orders from anyone, including God; they want to take part in God's decision-making process (to BE the Furrow of His Brow). Reverend Misner takes their side. Steward Morgan, furious, says:

> *"If you, any one of you, ignore, change, take away, or add to the words in the mouth of that Oven, I will blow your head off just like you was a hood-eye snake."*

The women in *Paradise* are more interesting than the men, but there are times when all the good citizens of Ruby seem like the *Stepford Wives* (and *Husbands*). Deek's wife Soane often seems on the verge of an epiphany—the agonized dignity over the death of her sons, the gentle strength with which she handles her husband's affair—but she never quite makes it. Her sister, Steward's wife Dovey, isn't at all intimidated by her badass husband, but Steward comes to life only in his boyishly romantic love for her.

Divine

The next section, Divine, is partly about the fourth "guest" to turn up at the Convent. Her name is Pallas. She hurts so bad she can barely talk—16 years old and rendered silent by bad love. The section opens in 1974, at the wedding of K.D. and Arnette. Although they are to be married by sporty young Reverend Misner, the ceremony opens with a brutal sermon by the old fire-and-brimstoner, Reverend Pulliam, who asks, basically, *What makes you so arrogant that you think that God is interested in you?* Misner realizes that Pulliam's accusatory sermon is directed at him and is so rattled that he spends the next five pages examining his spiritual toothache while holding up a cross.

But that isn't the worst thing that happens that day: Soane, Deek's wife, makes the mistake of inviting the Convent women to K.D. and Arnette's wedding reception. The women pile out of

SUSPENSE in a novel is usually created by making the reader wonder what happens next in the story. In *Paradise*, however, Toni Morrison creates discrete little pockets of suspense by making us wonder who each section is named for. In the section titled "Grace," she makes us wait until the end to find out that Gigi's real name is Grace (then plays off the word "grace" for a bit of added magic). In the "Seneca" section, TM gives a long rap on the citizens of Ruby before even mentioning Seneca, and then messes with our minds by inviting us to confuse Seneca with Sweetie. In "Divine," when TM finally spills the beans about who Divine is—Pallas' boyfriend-stealing mother—we are a bit disappointed. (Later, TM turns that disappointment into something beautiful.)

CHRONOLOGY (dates approximate)

1880s—158 freedmen, led by Old Fathers, leave Mississippi and Louisiana to establish their own town.

1889—79 people, including Big Papa and Big Daddy, get lost outside Fairly, Oklahoma.

1890—The Old Fathers establish HAVEN in Oklahoma Territory and build the Oven.

1905—Haven grows to 1000 citizens.

1910—Haven has two churches and a Bank; Big Daddy drives around to check out other Colored towns.

1922—The Convent is built.

1924—Deacon and Steward Morgan are born.

1932—Haven is thriving, unaffected by the Depression.

1934—Haven is reduced to 500 citizens, 200, then 80.

the Cadillac and start partying. Reverend Pulliam declares that the fun-obsessed adults are a sign that the world is going to hell. The Convent women are thrown out of the wedding reception and, on the ride back to the Convent, Mavis and Gigi get into a fight. As the chapter ends, Mavis is talking to her dead twins.

The chaos of names at this point in the book is so overwhelming that a genealogy of all the characters seems necessary to keep track. WHOOPS!—the novel, which suddenly seems to have a mind of its own, gallops off in another direction!

Patricia

You've heard of a shaggy-dog story? The sixth section, "Patricia," is named for Pat Best—a schoolteacher working on the town's genealogy— and might be called a shaggy-ancestor story. Pat has been working on the genealogy for years, borrowing family Bibles, asking questions, and investigating gossip. Patricia finally concludes that, since people lie about who they have sex with, any genealogy is doomed from the start—*so she burns all her papers!*

1942—Deek and Steward enlist in the Army.

1949—15 families leave Haven to start over.

1950—The New Fathers found RUBY; Ruby Morgan dies.

1964—Soane's baby aborts; Steward and Dovey learn they can't have kids.

1968—Mavis arrives at the Convent.

1969—Scout and Easter Morgan killed in Vietnam.

1970—Rev. Misner comes to Calvary church; Gigi comes to town and goes to the Convent.

1973—Argument over the Oven; Seneca arrives at Convent.

1974—Pallas arrives at Convent; KD and Arnette get married.

1976—The men of Ruby attack the Convent.

While trying to figure out why some of the community's original families were no longer counted among the town's "holy families," Patricia realizes how people had been ranked in Haven and Ruby since the beginning: they would remain God's Chosen People only as long as they kept their 8-Rock blood untainted. Anyone who mated with a light-skinned person or had light-skinned children relinquished the racial purity on which their identity was based.

"Everything that worries them," Patricia realized, "must come from women."

Consolata

The seventh section, "Consolata," is the given name of Connie, the steadfast but dull woman who runs the Convent. Years before they came to the Convent, during a tour of duty in Brazil, the nuns had stolen a child from the slums of Rio. They raised the stolen child, Consolata, as if she were one of them. For her first 30 years in the Convent, Consolata devoted herself to God. Then one day she sees Deek Morgan:

> He was twenty-nine. She was thirty-nine. And she lost her mind. Completely.

This is the most interesting section in the book: love, lust, instant transformation—all magic and no realism—as she meets Deek's twin and his wife, and is "tricked into raising the dead." Connie undergoes another transformation, becoming sort of the guru at a spiritual girl scouts camp.

Lone

The eighth section is called "Lone," after Lone DuPres, the old midwife and magic woman who drove out to the Convent in the middle of the night to warn the women. The chapter describes in more detail the slaughter that opened the book. The last page of the chapter describes either a supernatural occurrence or somebody's attempt to make it look like one.

Save-Marie

The ninth section, "Save-Marie," is the name of one of Jeff and Sweetie Fleetwood's sickly children. The setting is Save-Marie's funeral. The chapter expands to show how each of the characters tell the story of the slaughter of the Convent women—and how the town reacts to it. The story ends with ... no, let's leave that for you to discover!

How did the critics react to *Paradise*?

On the surface, the first wave of critics didn't seem to agree on anything—not even the subject of the first line (*"They shoot the white girl first"*). Writing in *The New York Times Book Review*, Brooke Allen identified her as *"Pallas, a ... privileged white girl whose ... parents have failed her miserably."* In *The New Yorker*, Louis Menand referred to her as *"Seneca, a white runaway...."*

Some critics thought the book was wonderful. Allen wrote:

> It is possibly her best work of fiction to date. ... Morrison has brought it all together: the poetry, the emotion, the symbolic plan.

Others, like David Gates of *Newsweek*, thought it was lame.

> [W]e're asked to swallow too many contrivances: the cultists' hangout was originally a decadent mansion with pornographic bathroom fixtures and then a Roman Catholic convent; the transformation of the cult leader Consolata from a lush to a charismatic guru is more convenient than convincing.

On the other hand, virtually all the critics had the same blind spots, jumping to the same mistaken conclusions. They all thought that what they saw on the surface was what *Paradise* is really about. Michiko Kakutani's review in *The New York Times* is a case in point, calling it:

> a heavy-handed .... contrived, formulaic book that mechanically pits men against women, old against young, the past against the present.
>
> Nearly every one of [the] characters is a two-dimensional cliché...
>
> There are gratuitous Biblical allusions (like comparing the story of Ruby's founders to the story of the Holy Family, turned away from the inn) and even more gratuitous suggestions that the women at the convent are feminist martyrs, like the witches of Salem.

But consider the possibility that all the bad little things Kakutani accused TM of are part of a brilliantly constructed piece of literary mischief.

Start with this: "comparing the story of Ruby's founders to the story of the Holy Family, turned away at the inn" might qualify as "a gratuitous Biblical allusion" if there were only ONE Holy Family. But didn't Ms. Kakutani notice that there were SEVEN

Holy Families in the novel? Did it not occur to her that seven Holy Families is so preposterous that the comparison isn't "gratuitous"— it's *ridiculous*! Where's her sense of humor?

And then there's this monumental misunderstanding: "Nearly every one of [the] characters is a two-dimensional cliché." Ms. Kakutani, were you really bothered by the fact that *Paradise*'s characters are not realistic? Mavis, whose twins gave her no trouble (*but died in her Cadillac* while she was shopping in *Higgledy Piggledy*) escapes with "*canary-yellow feet*" (her daughter's boots) and drops by to see her mother, *Birdie Goodroe,* while *Seneca* goes to *Wichita* to see *Eddie Turtle*'s mother and work for *Norma Fox*!!!—simple, rhyming, and goofy as a nursery rhyme!

Not realistic? *No shit, Sherlock! Paradise*'s characters are not real because Morrison didn't intend them to be. The plot isn't realistic because TM *wanted* it to be over the top—like a myth! In fact, she uses the novel to try out every kind of myth one can think of, from Biblical and Greek to witch hunts and cartoons.

Paradise does things it doesn't seem possible for a novel to do. The first wave of reviewers fell into Morrison's trap, missing important clues and overlooking her great sense of humor. Even more astonishing is the fact that critics and scholars who have had years to understand *Paradise* are no closer to the heart of the book than the original coven of reviewers. *Paradise* is Morrison's most misunderstood work.

What *Paradise* is REALLY About

In one of the most ingenious strategies by any novelist ever, Toni Morrison uses *Paradise* to show how oral history, written history, myth—and Truth itself—overlap and trip over each other. Her purpose is not just to *tell* us about those critical misjudgments, but to *show* us that we make the same mistakes without even noticing it. Everything from the slaughter of the "nuns" to the cartoon characters are perfectly designed pieces in a brilliantly subversive Trickster Novel.

Paradise is not a "feminist novel" or a "racial novel." It is a myth-in-progress about reality, mythology, and God. Every people's history begins as oral history and evolves (or not) into written history. Not only is *Paradise* <u>about</u> myth, it IS a myth. The form of the novel is as mythological as its content.

As part of her method, Morrison makes silly, intentional "mistakes" and defies us to notice them...

Like: In the legendary first journey of their ancestors, *"one hundred and fifty-eight freedmen"* left and *"all seventy-nine were lost."*

Like: Steward Morgan, the twin who remembers "every detail" of everything, refers to "walking pneumonia" as "*locking* pneumonia." (Is the town genius really a bozo?)

Like: "They kill the white girl first"—but no one knows who the white girl is.

Like: Needing a palm leaf cross and sunglasses to kill the girls.

After reading *Paradise*, you may feel as if you know more about the citizens of Ruby, Oklahoma, than you've known about the characters of any book. **But beware!** While you *can* recite an endless list of facts, what you *cannot* do is put them together in any sensible way. Take the collapse of Haven. The town was founded in 1890 and collapsed in 1934, after the men came home from World War II. **But wait!** World War II ended in 1945!

What's Going on Here?

Everybody makes mistakes. One person sees things differently from another person, interprets things differently, remembers things differently. And most people lie occasionally. Morrison isn't going to take us by the hand and tell us who's doing what, so we have to pay attention.

Tricks, traps, and treats are planted throughout the novel. The moment you discover even one of them, you become Morrison's co-conspirator. One of her main goals is to bring you (the reader) so far into the novel that, in a manner of speaking, *you help her write it.* That moment of discovery—when you share a secret with the author—is one of the most thrilling experiences a reader can have.

Example: In the section "Her Work: Reinventing the Novel," it was suggested that the **names** in Morrison's novels merit special attention. In *Paradise*, the name "Seneca" is a perfect example. If you did some background reading, you'd find something like this:

SENECA

Seneca was a Roman philosopher, statesman, and author in the 1st century C.E. He created a genre of literature known as the Senecan tragedies, a body of nine "closet dramas"—intended to be read rather than acted. (*Paradise* has nine Patriarchs, nine Founding Families, and nine killers; it is constructed in nine sections named after nine women.) When Seneca's tragedies were rediscovered in the 16th century, few people in Renaissance Europe had ever seen the original Greek plays, so they thought that Seneca's were the real thing. Seneca's reworkings of dramas by Euripides, Aeschylus, and Sophocles became the models for a revival of Greek tragedy during the Renaissance.

But Seneca's plays differ from the originals in several respects: a moralizing and pompous rhetoric, a focus on horrible deeds, and more static characters who tend to rant. As such, they represent a different approach to writing—and to life—than the original Greek versions. If you're interested in the difference, read the argument in *Paradise* between Reverend Pulliam and Reverend Misner. Here's the short version:

Greek tragedy presented a world believed to be just and rational. When things got tough, you could ask the gods for help and sometimes they would come through. In the end, one way or the other, you always got what you deserved ... even if you had to give it to yourself.

Senecan tragedy presented a world in which only an idiot expects reason or fairness. Seneca's plays all end with a tirade that says essentially what the fire-breathing Reverend Pulliam says: *What makes you so damned arrogant that you think the gods are interested in you?*

Aside from providing some fascinating information on an important literary figure, allusions such as this bring historical and theological clarity to themes of the novel, to critics' reactions, and to the author's intention.

Morrison does nothing by accident, nor is there one and only one layer to her truth. There is certainly room for debate as to how we should read *Paradise*, but it's clear that we should *not* read it either straight or carelessly. But what's the point of all these cartoon characters, mythical gods, out-of-whack facts, and other literary sleights of hand? How does it all connect?

Paradise is a myth about the tug-of-war war between myth and truth, storytelling and reality. Myopic academic interpretations (the ones that miss the humor) say it's the difference between oral history and written history. Written history is usually considered more accurate than oral history—especially by the group that wrote it. Among other things, *Paradise* makes the point that African Americans have never been in a position to write their own history. To TM, a people's history is an essential part of their identity. So when she says **"Our past has been appropriated. I am one of the people who has to reappropriate it,"** *she means it, completely and literally.*

Paradise is a myth about how myths are formed, changed, and de-formed. Since myth is part of a people's oral history, everything in it has to be extreme, larger than life, exaggerated. Good Guys vs. Bad Guys, easy to remember and cartoon clear. But knowing Toni Morrison, there's more going on than cartoons…

Who's Telling This Story ... and Why Are They Screwing It Up?

When a writer like Morrison inserts a foolish mathematical error ("over twice the number of women") on Page One, she's setting off an alarm. She wants to wake us up. But what is she trying to tell us? Who is making the mistake and why?

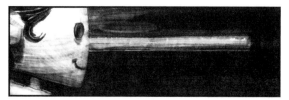

Morrison originally said that she had conceived of *Beloved, Jazz,* and *Paradise* as a trilogy.

She later retracted the statement—then retracted the retraction(!) ... so the trilogy is back in play. *Beloved. Jazz. Paradise.* All connected. How does this help us understand *Paradise*?

Two of the last things that happened in *Jazz* were Felice telling Joe about the apple—a reference to the Garden of Eden, or Paradise; and Felice telling Joe and Violet about her "unusual" friendship with Dorcas—a friendship between a light-skinned African American girl and a dark-skinned one, the same problem the Founding Fathers faced.

Thus, in a sense, *Paradise* begins where *Jazz* left off. The most notable thing about *Jazz*'s ending was its bizarre Narrator. It sounded like God in Her Hair Rollers over a cup of coffee—but It made mistakes, got things wrong, couldn't be trusted. So on Page One of *Paradise*, TM is telling us that this novel, too, has a narrator who makes mistakes and can't be trusted.

Next Question: About this Narrator who opens the book and gets things wrong—*Who is it?* Toni Morrison or God? Maybe it's both. Maybe TM isn't saying that THIS narrator is unreliable, but that ALL narrators are unreliable. Including herself.

Conversely, Morrison also seems to be saying that whatever information we're given, we interpret. As psychologists and criminal defense lawyers have long said: all eyewitnesses are unreliable. In the last chapter of *Paradise*, everyone, including the people who witnessed the slaughter, has a different story. Even the trustworthy Lone DuPres has reconstructed the slaughter so that it adds up to something coherent not only in its own right, but with the rest of her life (*If only I had followed my instincts about the birds at KD's wedding…*).

As TM put it when describing the people in *Beloved*, we "deconstruct reality" and then "reconstruct" it until it fits, no matter what we have to add, subtract, change, or ignore. That's the way we construct our myths, the way we construct our pasts, and the way we construct our everyday "reality." So what TM does in *Paradise* is at once underhanded and ingenious: she rigs the novel so that the critics not only complete it, but they actually prove its thesis—even while denying it! If that sounds impossible, consider the following.

The opening of *Paradise*, no matter how repulsed you are by the slaughter, is so arresting that most reviewers quoted the first two paragraphs. Although good critics are some of the smartest people on the planet, it isn't fair to expect them to connect a few facts separated by 200 pages. Yet virtually every reviewer, after quoting the opening passages—*inside the reviews that they themselves wrote*—went on to say that the shooters killed FIVE women. None of them noticed the mathematical idiocy (that nine is NOT "over twice" FIVE). They had so thoroughly "reconstructed" reality that they incorporated incompatible "facts" into their own reviews! Thus, they complete Morrison's novel by proving her thesis right before our eyes: *We do whatever we must to make sense of the world, even if it takes turning so dumb in one little square inch of our lives that it never occurs to us that nine isn't more than "twice five."*

OK: That's what *Paradise* DOES.
But what does *Paradise* MEAN?

Reconnecting the Trilogy

TM has said she started with the intention of making *Beloved*, *Jazz*, and *Paradise* a trilogy in which each of the books is about a certain kind of love taken to excess.

- *Beloved* is about love of one's children taken to excess.

- *Jazz* is about romantic love taken to excess.

- *Paradise* is about love of God taken to excess.

Translated into *action,* the first two statements might be reformulated as follows:

- I love my daughter so much that under certain circumstances I would kill her.

- I love that woman so much that under certain circumstances I would kill her.

But when it comes to God, the notion of excessive love is usually understood to mean:

- I love God so much that I would kill people who don't believe in Him.

This last statement is way out of symmetry with the first two—and far too vanilla for the fiercely original Morrison. To make her "love of God" statement symmetrical with the others, you'd have to say:

- I love God so much that under certain circumstances I would kill Him.

BUT WAIT! Even this statement is not quite symmetrical with the first two, is it? Maybe we miss the heart of *Paradise* unless we make TM's three love/kill statements *perfectly* symmetrical:

- I love my daughter so much that under certain circumstances I would kill her.

- I love that woman so much that under certain circumstances I would kill her.

- I love God so much that under certain circumstances I would kill Her.

Seriously. Some of the most intense arguments about the meaning of *Paradise* were about the gender of God—or the gods. The good citizens of Ruby did not kill any "hims," they killed five "hers." What if the heart and soul of *Paradise* is not the town of Ruby or Haven or the Founding Fatheads? What if it's really the Convent? What if *Paradise* is not the story of the men's mythology, but the *women's*?

Figuring Out the Epigraph

A novel's epigraph is usually the first place you look to get a handle

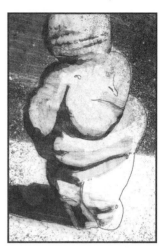

on the book's meaning, but *Paradise*'s epigraph is not only vague, it is unattributed—TM didn't say where she took it from. She could have written it herself. Did any of the book reviews figured out the epigraph? To look find out, I first went back to John Leonard's epic review of *Jazz*. "Her Soul's High Song" (*The Nation*, May 25, 1992) to look for "clues." Leonard described the epigraph to *Jazz*:

> **Picking up on the epigraph to Jazz—from "Thunder, Perfect Mind" in The Nag Hammadi—and knowing that Morrison now spends part of every week at Princeton with Elaine Pagels, who wrote the book on the Gnostic Gospels, I said, "Aha!" "Thunder: Perfect Mind" is the revelation of a feminine power: "I am the whore, and the holy one. I am the wife and the virgin."**

Wow! Not only did this confirm that TM had done some serious thinking about female gods, but it reminds us that many of the female gods were goddesses of fertility—sex gods!—which aligns perfectly with the fact the Convent started out as a porno playground. So I picked up a copy of Pagels' *Gnostic Gospels*, along with the full *Nag Hammadi* text. As suspected, the epigraph in *Paradise* was taken from "Thunder: Perfect Mind," the revelation of a feminine power.

BAM! No question about it: I was zeroing in on the center of the novel.

"The Thunder" and Other Perfect Minds
The powerful lines quoted by John Leonard are the high-point of "Thunder: Perfect Mind," but the quality of the verse is inconsequential in light of what it describes—namely, a "divine revelation" by a Christian female god. Not a saint, but a *god*. In the poem, the goddess draws parallels between herself and the gods of Greece and Egypt. By what she says, you can tell she's not the only god or even the top god in the pantheon; if there's a hierarchy, she's probably Number Two. *Incredible*—a polytheistic Christianity with a high-ranking female god (or gods)!

The Gnostics were among the earliest Christians, but we never knew much about them because orthodox Christians burned their writings. In 1945, however, an Egyptian peasant found dozens of Gnostic manuscripts in the village of Nag Hammadi on the banks of the Nile. The texts discovered there, dating from the 2nd to the 4th centuries C.E., provide a taste of what the Gnostics believed and what Christianity almost—but never—became.

One of the recurring questions about *Paradise* is whether it concerns female divinities—and what the implications of that are. Can the women in *Paradise* be considered goddesses or martyrs? They were obviously victims—but martyrs? Martyrhood doesn't seem to have any spitiual requirements—all you have to do is die. They certainly filled that requirement. *Goddesses?* That would be a stretch—except for Consolata. (*See* **Piedade** sidebar below.)

Is *Paradise* modeled on the Bible?

There are parallels, for sure. *Paradise*, like the Bible, has a huge cast of characters. After the Disallowing, the 8-Rocks consider themselves Chosen People. And the founder of Haven, Zechariah "Big Papa" Morgan, carries the same name as the Hebrew prophet who helped restore Israel after the departure from Babylon.

The whole novel is not modeled on the Bible, though there's no doubt that the 8-Rocks modeled their mythology on it. With apologies to those who can't abide the idea of a humorous Bible, at times *Paradise* seems like a slapstick version of the Good Book. The 8-Rocks modeled their myth on the Bible, but in an absurd way. Their slaughter of the Convent women has a self-righteous Biblical tone, not unlike the Old Testament Hebrew prophets.

Louis Menand (in the *New Yorker*) quipped, "but did it have to have *four* resurrections?" (There were really five.) And when the

New Founders put on a Christmas play with *seven* Holy Families, it was hilarious!

Was *Paradise* actually critical of the Bible? TM seems to have noticed with a vengeance that the Bible is, after all, the scripture of White Eurocentric Male Mythology. Given the high regard for Christianity she'd shown in the past, it would be surprising to see her so critical of it here. But given her zero tolerance for White Eurocentric Male *anything*, it's surprising that it took her so long.

Reappropriating the Past

Morrison's novels often have more than one "center." Does *Paradise* have another underlying theme that combines the pieces into a single unified whole?

Yes: *Paradise* plugs into one of the central projects of Toni Morrison's life as a writer: "reappropriating her people's past." One of the ways she approaches the task is by using fiction to explore different ways of dealing with it. Just as the three books in Morrison's trilogy are about three different kinds of love taken to excess, they're also about three different ways of dealing with the past:

- *Beloved* is about trying to FORGET or repress the past.

- *Jazz* is about trying to IGNORE or skip over the past.

- *Paradise* is about REINVENTING or rewriting the past.

Is Consolata a Goddess?

One of Toni Morrison's favorite writers, Gabriel García Márquez, is a celebrated Colombian novelist known for a narrative style called "magical realism." In Toni Morrison's view, magical realism is inherently part of the African American experience as well—so she included it as one of the defining characteristics of the African American novel

Mythologist Joseph Campbell had some interesting things to say about the evolution of Jesus. Campbell said

JOSEPH CAMPBELL

that most cultures had Gods who were gentle, loving, and if need be, willing to sacrifice themselves for their people. In Campbell's view, one of the unique aspects of Jesus was that he was a male. So had Christianity taken a typical female God and turned Her into a male. And did TM turn him back into a woman?

The Gnostic approach to answering that question is elegant and infinitely tolerant. The Gnostics categorically rejected the notion that anyone can explain God or Christ or the religious experience to you. They saw God as a personal spiritual Experience that can only be known directly, one-on-one. I see God in one way, you see God in whatever way He, She, It or They appear to you.

God is Your Experience of God.

And Morrison's *Paradise* is **YOUR Experience of *Paradise*.**

With all that said, let's have a go at the Big Question.

Is God the Ultimate Unreliable Narrator?

TM certainly seems to be implying that. After Consolata brings a dead person back to life, she prays because she thinks she has offended God. Lone DuPres, her "adviser," tells her to stop being a wuss and do what God wants. Consolata answers, "I think He wants me to ignore you."

And what about the endless arguments between the preachers (or within Reverend Misner himself)? Is Morrison saying that even if there IS only One God, He is such an Unreliable Narrator that we don't know if He's a Baptist, Methodist, Pentecostal, Catholic, Candomblé-ist, Jew, Muslim, Buddhist, Feminist or Trickster God who wants to drive us all crazy!

154

Or should we put it like Danish philosopher Soren Kierkegaard did: No matter what God tells you, YOU have to decide if the voice you hear is the Real God or a False God or the Devil or One God Among Many? Whether God is an Unreliable Narrator or we are Unreliable Interpreters, it amounts to the same thing: God doesn't make our choices—we do.

KoKoPELLi

And so, in the end, what TM seems to be doing is playing—or being—the Trickster Goddess, teasing us, fooling us, coming to "inconclusive conclusions".

Paradise is about reading carefully and skeptically. Reading books, life, God, each other's humanity, name it. It's about refusing to go blind in any square inch of your life.

Paradise is a Trickster Bible, a Gnostic Novel, a myth about folks whose myth is busted but don't even know it until some mythical goddess appears and writes a mythical book about folks whose myth is busted but don't even know it until some mythical goddess appears and writes a mythical book...

Paradise is one of the most original novels ever written.

LATER NOVELS
(2003–2015)

Toni Morrison has written four novels since *Paradise*. There isn't room in a book this size to treat the later works in the same detail we have treated her first seven novels, but it would be out of the question to ignore them.

Do we analyze Morrison's later novels collectively or individually?

We will treat the later works briefly and somewhat collectively, followed by truncated descriptions of each novel. The later novels are *Love* (2003), *A Mercy* (2008), *Home* (2012), and *God Help the Child* (2015).

If you have all four books in front of you, the first thing you notice is that the later works are much smaller that TM's earlier novels. *Love*, the first of the later novels, is barely 200 pages long—and it's the longest of the four books.

Thematically, the later novels are consistent with TM's earlier work. They address her grand themes: slavery; the past's stranglehold on the present; the individual's relationship to the community; respect for ancestors, etc. But her approach in the newer novels is in many ways surprising, unpredictable, and oblique.

Perhaps the most blatant example of TM's new take on an old

theme is found in *A Mercy*, set in colonial Virginia during the late 17th century, "a place before slavery was equated with race." The de-racializing of slavery demands an approach very different from TM's impassioned dissection of the subject during the Civil War era. *A Mercy* includes Native American slaves, Portuguese slaves, white slaves, 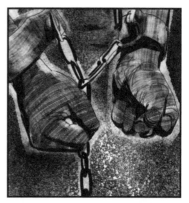 indentured servants, and free Black men—enslaved and oppressed people of every imaginable background, including European women whose career choices were threefold: servant, prostitute, or wife.

Stylistically, TM's later works are variations of the split-narrative style she developed in her mature earlier work—the stories are divided among several different characters. But the later books are more straightforward. Despite their surprising elements, the new novels have become progressively more accessible, easier to read and understand.

TM's later works fill the gaps, both geographically and chronologically, between (and before) her earlier novels: *A Mercy* is set in 17th-century America; *Home*: a soldier's journey from California to Georgia, takes place after the Korean War. *God Help the Child* is set in modern-day California.

It may or may not be hyperbole to say that Toni Morrison singlehandedly "reappropriated her people's history"... but she certainly left one hell of a footprint.

Love
(2003)

Love, Morrison's eighth novel, is the only one of her later works that reads like a TM novel as we've come to understand it so far. The writing is lush and unignorable. The novel consists of a prologue and nine chapters in which different characters tell the story of Bill Cosey, the owner of Cosey's Hotel and Resort, off the coast of North Carolina.

Every woman in the novel "displaces herself" so completely that the only parts of their lives that have meaning were their relationships to Cosey. Even the book's chapters are named for their relationships to him: Friend, Stranger, Benefactor, Lover, Husband, Guardian, Father, Phantom. Together the novel's nine "split narrative" chapters cover the period from Jim Crow segregation to Civil Rights and desegregation—in other words, from the 1930s to the 1990s. TM's take on everything from Martin Luther King, Jr., to Malcolm X and 1960s "revolutionaries" is original and often comic.

Bill Cosey starts out as the most exemplary male character in any Toni Morrison novel. A tone of over-the-top adoration permeates the first half of the book. Cosey is a devastatingly handsome, incredibly generous entrepreneur. His Hotel and Resort, catering exclusively to wealthy African Americans, thrives even during the Depression. What a man!

> *He liked George Raft clothes and gangster cars, but he used his heart like Santa Claus. If a family couldn't pay for a burial, he had a quiet talk with the undertaker. He took care of a stroke victim's doctor bills and his granddaughter's college fees.*

And he was an exemplary father. His only demand on his son, Billy Boy, was that he "had to be interesting." Cosey took his son everywhere.

> *[He] wanted Billy Boy to see men enjoying the perfection of their work, so they went to Perdido Street for King Oliver, Memphis for the Tigers. They watched cooks, bartenders, pickpockets. Everything was a labor lesson from a man proud of his skill.*

But then Billy Boy dies. Morrison never explicitly connects cause and effect, but from that moment on the novel's depiction of Cosey becomes less adoring, more critical. His drinking becomes less playful and more needy. His generosity becomes less gracious, more like renting friends. And in his womanizing, he is less the adored prince and more the dirty old man. Although Cosey has been dead for 20 years when the novel opens, he is still at the center of it.

And then he isn't.

At first, everyone is blinded by the light of Cosey's magnificence. You may not even notice that the novel is building "like a crystal" around two women, Christine and Heed. Both in their sixties, they live in Cosey's old Monarch Street house and, when they have the energy, fight over ownership of the house. (It's the old missing will story.) Christine and Heed were best friends as children, but then Cosey married Heed. Now, 20 years after Cosey's death, they are sworn enemies who live on different floors of the same house. Heed, *"a high-heeled snake,"* posts an ad for a "personal assistant" (to help her fake a will), while *"Christine, true to her whore's heart, sporting diamonds in their rightful owner's face, was pilfering house money to pay a lawyer."*

Cover your ears while I mention that Heed was 11 years old when Cosey married her. (In this book, Morrison's magic is easier to believe than her realism.) By the time the novel ends, many readers will have lost interest in the Gothic baloney about the missing will, but will eagerly continue reading for the sheer pleasure of TM's writing.

Morrison's later novels play off her earlier characters and themes.

Heed and Christine echo Sula and Nel. *Love* begins with Romen, a 14-year-old hardbody, and Junior Viviane, a streetwise young lady who shows up in a miniskirt and no underwear. (Another nod to *Sula*!) The only chapter in *Love* not named for Bill Cosey's relationship with someone else, is "Portrait"—a painting of Cosey. The portrait, hanging in the old Monarch Street house, is like a reverse *Portrait of Dorian Gray*. It doesn't show the ravages of age and corruption; instead it embodies the spirit of Cosey himself, charming and overheating Junior, becoming a third-party participant in Junior's and Romen's moderately sadomasochistic sex.

(Even in death, Bill Cosey is still *The Man*!)

Thematically, *Love* plays devil's advocate to the harsh judgment Morrison expressed to Gail Caldwell in their conversation about *Beloved*: "*What was on my mind was the way in which women are so vulnerable to displacing themselves into something other than themselves*," she said then. In the same way, every woman in *Love* "displaces herself" completely, deferring to the needs of Bill Cosey.

Much as Morrison's later works echo or comment on her earlier works, there seems to be a real anomaly in which a later work points toward an *even later* later work. In *Love* (2003), she writes: "*Overblown names people give to mules and fishing boats. Bride. Welcome Morning. Princess Starlight.*" But note that Bride is the very "overblown name" that the main character in *God Save the Child* (2015) gives herself! And the description of Heed, Cosey's 11-year-old bride, is almost exactly the same as that of Bride, reverting to the pre-adolescent (no breasts, no pubic hair) version of herself. *Whatever game Toni Morrison is playing here, you gotta love it!*

Nor is Morrison given enough credit for her raunchy sense of humor. How about this, from *Love*:

> **[B]eing the daughter of a preacher, she really tried to dredge up Christian charity, but failed whenever she looked at a Johnson.**

Morrison, who knows the nuances of African American street lingo as well as anyone, knows that a "Johnson" is slang for the male sex organ.

A Mercy
(2008)

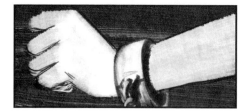

Of all her works, *A Mercy* reads the least like a Morrison novel in both style and content. Especially compared to her earlier novels, it is conspicuously minimalist in style. The language is more condensed than in her previous books, yet it's often so pure and elemental that it feels like she's invented the language. Although *A Mercy* is "about" slavery, it runs counter to TM's usual stance on the subject. The book jacket for the first edition describes the novel as "a prelude to [*Beloved*], set two centuries earlier."

In the 1680s the slave trade was still in its infancy. In the Americas, virulent religious and class divisions, prejudice and oppression were rife, providing the fertile soil in which slavery and race hatred were planted and took hold.

Morrison's surprising and unique intent in this novel is, as she put it, to "remove race from slavery." The novel's cast of characters includes D'Ortega, a conscience-free Portuguese slave trader, and Jacob Vaark, an Anglo-Dutch trader trying to build a better life in the New World. Although Vaark is repulsed by slavery, he reluctantly accepts Florens, a Portuguese-African slave girl, in exchange for a bad debt. Lina, a Native American slave whose tribe was decimated by measles, takes on the role of Florens' surrogate mother. They are joined by Rebekka, Vaark's London mail-order bride, and a strange girl named Sorrow.

Although Vaark detests D'Ortega, he becomes obsessed with D'Ortega's huge house. Vaark had started out as a farmer but lacked the temperament for it and began trafficking in rum. He realized that he was becoming part of the molasses-rum-slaves triangle, a business every bit as brutal as the slave trade, but he was doing well financially and expanded his business. A short time later, however, his infant sons and daughter die. Numbed by grief, Vaark begins building a mansion of his own, for which he envisions an ornate metal gate. He hires a free African metalworker, referred to only as the blacksmith, to build his wrought iron gate.

For a while, the women become as close to a family as any of them have ever known. Then Vaark dies of smallpox. After surviving the deaths of all four of her children, and now her husband, Rebekka falls gravely ill. She orders Florens to find the blacksmith, who has a reputation as a healer—and whom Florens has fallen madly in love with. The blacksmith, who has never been anyone's slave, knows he is equal or superior to anyone on earth. He breaks Florens' heart by telling her that her love for him has made her a slave: *"Own yourself, woman."*

This sets the stage for the novel's most famous fancy talk. If they ever decide to publish a line of Intellectual Literary Fortune Cookies, this will surely be on it:

> **To be given dominion over another is a hard thing; to wrest dominion over another is a wrong thing; to give dominion of yourself to another is a wicked thing.**

Structurally, *A Mercy* is divided into 12 chapters, six of which are narrated by Florens—all told as first-person narratives: *I* did this, *I* saw that. Her story "glues" the chapters together. Each of the other six chapters is about one of the other characters, described by a nameless third-person narrator. The 12 chapters are not identified in the novel, and it helps to know who's speaking. Here's a summary:

Chapter	Begin page*	Point of View	Opening words
1	3	Florens	*Don't be afraid. My telling can't hurt you...*
2	9	Jacob Vaark	*The man moved through the surf...*
3	36	Florens	*Since your leaving ...*
4	43	Lina	*Lina was unimpressed by the festive...*
5	67	Florens	*Night is thick no stars anyplace...*
6	72	Rebekka	*How long will it take...*
7	101	Florens	*I sleep then wake to any sound.*
8	116	Sorrow	*She did not mind when they called her Sorrow...*
9	135	Florens	*My journey to you is hard and long...*
10	143	Willard & Scully	*Jacob Vaark climbed out of his grave...*
11	157	Florens	*I walk the night through.*
12	162	Florens' mother	*Neither one will want your brother.*

*Original hardcover edition.

The novel contains some wonderful little vignettes, set pieces, and asides:

- Rebekka in London: her "career choices" were "servant, prostitute, or wife" (not that there was much difference between them at the time.)

- Rebekka's boat trip to America: "I shat among strangers for six weeks to get to this land."

- A brief fictional account of Bacon's Rebellion, in which black slaves and white indentured servants joined forces to overthrow the governor of Virginia in 1676. The laws of the time allowed any white person to kill any black, Native American, or servant without legal consequences of any kind.

- The portrayal of Willard and Scully, indentured servants who worked for the Vaarks. They were a gay couple who survived together and were an integral part of the Vaark's makeshift family.

Underscoring her theme of the pre-racial roots of slavery, Morrison observed the following in an interview with National Public Radio:

> *"Every civilization in the world relied on [slavery]. The only difference between African slaves and European or British slaves was that the latter could run away and melt into the population."*

Florens, the novel's central character uses the phrase *"minha mae"* several times. John Updike, in his notoriously cranky review of *A Mercy*, tells us that the phrase is Portuguese for "Mother." Updike's review, which deserves far more credit than it gets, concludes as follows:

A Mercy begins where it ends, with a white man casually answering a slave mother's plea, but he dies, and she fades into slavery's myriads, and the child goes mad with love. Varied and authoritative and frequently beautiful though the language is, it circles around a vision, both turgid and static, of a new world turning old, and poisoned from the start.

—John Updike, *The New Yorker*

A Mercy made the *New York Times Book Review* list of "Ten Best Books of 2008."

Home
(2012)

Home, Toni Morrison's tenth novel—and the third of her later works—is yet another surprising departure. Instead of broadening her focus, as she did in *A Mercy,* TM goes in the opposite direction and gives a brief, intense close-up of one tortured man. The main character, Frank Money,

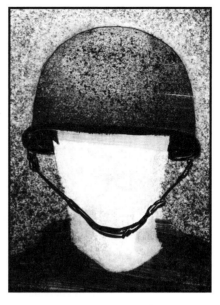

is back from the war in Korea. He has been discharged from the desegregated Army and returns to still-segregated America. A year after his discharge, Frank is still wandering the streets of Seattle, "not totally homeless, but close." He has gambled away his Army pay, lost odd jobs and a decent girlfriend, and awakes in a psyche ward for reasons he can't recall. His "free-floating rage" and "self-loathing" are symptoms of what we now call "post-traumatic stress disorder," but there was no such diagnosis at the time. Frank Money was just a pissed-off, six-foot-three-inch Black man, and he didn't get a lot of sympathy.

Stuck in a psych ward without his shirt or boots, he forces himself to remember an unsigned letter he'd been given that said only,

"Come fast. She be dead if you tarry."

Frank has no idea who "she" is or what the letter means. He sneaks out of the nut house as quickly as he can, then runs barefoot in the snow to a nearby church he had noticed from the back seat of the patrol car. The parson gives him food, clothing, and the money from the collection box. It came to seventeen dollars, enough to get Frank the hell out of Seattle.

Thirty pages later Frank has a dream insinuating that the mysterious letter was about his sister, Cee. Cee was the person he'd selflessly cared for more than anyone in the world. She was the one who'd be dead if he tarried. And so, fast as he can, he makes his way toward Lotus, Georgia. Home: the place hated more than anyplace in the world. Frank and two homeboys, both of whom died grotesquely in Korea, had joined the Army to get out of Lotus.

As we've come to expect from TM's novels, the narration jumps from person to person and present to past. The storytelling

in *Home* is split between Frank, Cee, and Frank's girlfriend, Lily. Frank's first-person voice (in italics) either begins or ends almost every chapter. Frank and Cee had brutal childhoods, due partly to small-town Georgia racism and partly to the mean upbringing of their grandmother, Lenore.

Backstory: Cee marries a slippery young man who "borrows" grandma's car and dumps Cee in a nearby town. Rather than face the embarrassment of going back to Lotus, Cee finds a place to live and takes a job as a domestic servant to a doctor. She's too naïve to be alarmed by the doctor's creepy questions and "scientific" books on race and eugenics. The degenerate doctor performs so many "scientific" operations on Cee that she ends up nearly dead.

Frank, meanwhile, hates Lotus: *"Only my sister in trouble could force me to even think about going in that direction."*

The mature women in Lotus nurse Cee back to health. She, alive and well but permanently unable to have children, begins to cry.

"Come on, girl. Don't cry," whispered Frank.
"Why not? I can be miserable if I want to. You don't need to try and make it go away. It shouldn't. It's just as sad as it ought to be..."

Frank admires his sister's willingness to face reality, no matter how brutal. He tries to match her courage, but his revelations about Korea are excruciating to him and to the reader. Not only is Frank breaking down, but the novel itself feels like it's cracking at the seams. It should be clear by now Morrison's novels are not fancy literary Flash Dances—they go straight to the fractured soul of the person expressing them. In *Home*, Frank Money is so distressed and desperate to be understood that he literally "comes out of the book" and speaks directly to the author:

Earlier you wrote about how sure I was that the beat up man on the train to Chicago would turn around and whip the wife who tried to help him. Not true. I didn't think any such thing.... I don't think you know much about love.
Or me.

Frank wants Toni Morrison to express *exactly* how he feels—and he will settle for nothing less. Toward the end of the book, TM's split narrative splits even further. Frank's point of view fractures, then fractures again. He's argues with the author—bitching out Toni Morrison!—for not getting his story exactly right.

"You can keep writing, but I think you ought to know what's true."

Published reviews of *Home* were uniformly quite positive, some literary in tone...

Ms. Morrison has found a new, angular voice and straight-ahead storytelling style that showcase ... her characters, and the ways in which violence and passion and regret are braided through their lives.
—Michiko Kakutani, The New York Times

And others steeped in reality...

As we watch this woefully damaged man try to find his way back into society, it is impossible not to think of the men and women who wear the uniform today.
—Tayari Jones, sfgate.com and the San Francisco Chronicle

God Help the Child
(2015)

God Help the Child—TM's eleventh novel and the fourth of her later works—finds its own style. It's far more effusive than *A Mercy*, but nowhere near as sumptuous as *Love*.

Thematically, *God Help the Child* is a fictional counterargument to an old theme: In *The Bluest Eye*, Beauty was poisonous. In *God Help the Child*, Beauty is ...what?

The opening lines of the novel are a real asskicker:

> **It's not my fault. So you can't blame me. I didn't do it and have no idea how it happened.**

What's not your fault? *What* can't we blame you for? *What* didn't you do, *for God's sake!?*

It's a great opening for a novel. It gets your juices flowing. You *need* answers to these questions. The person whose fault it isn't is a light-skinned Black woman who has just given birth to a very black baby. She is flabbergasted. Her family is light-skinned, her husband is light-skinned, and she has never been unfaithful. She really has no idea how it happened. She thinks about killing the baby, but does not. Her husband abandons her. She tells the growing child to call her Sweetness so no one will mistake her for the child's mother.

If Morrison's goal in *A Mercy* was to separate race from slavery, she goes a step further in *God Help the Child* by separating color from race.

Long story short: The ebony black child grows into a stunning beauty and becomes a famous model. Her visual signature is white clothing, posed against a white background (*"like a panther in the snow"*). Beautiful, savvy, and ambitious, she calls herself Bride and has her own line of cosmetics. She lives a life of High-Def glamour in Los Angeles.

WARNING: Beware of Queen Tut's curse! To be beautiful, successful, and wealthy early in a Toni Morrison novel is to invite disaster. Bride, at age 23, has the world in her beautiful ebony hands and falls in California love with Booker. They have good sex, barely know each other, and don't interfere with each other's lives. (Hey, it ain't Tristan and Isolde—it's modern day L.A.) One day, Booker, after an ambiguous five-word tirade, leaves.

Bride, at first too cool to give a damn, decides to take off on her own Booker-seeking Odyssey—with detours—that will change her life. But first she has unfinished business to take care of and meets a lady named Sofia Huxley on her release from prison. (To describe the situation any further would be a major spoiler, so let's leave it at that.) In any event...

- Bride, incapacitated after her meeting with Sofia Huxley, seems grateful when her assistant Brooklyn (a jive-talking white girl with dreadlocks) volunteers to cover for her at work.

- Bride resumes looking for Booker—she wants to know why he left her—and gets into a car wreck. She is rescued by a middle-aged hippie couple and their eccentric daughter, Rain.

- Bride re-resumes her erratic search for Booker and ends up in the home of Booker's aunt Queen. We learn that Booker had been a happy little boy until his brother Adam was killed by a child molester. Unable to forgive his family for trying to moving on with their lives after Adam's death, Booker left home. Queen was the only person who understood his angry need to keep grieving for his brother.

The novel then moves into a long, leisurely section about Booker. He was (and perhaps still is) an interesting young man: an aspiring

musician without great talent, and an aspiring intellectual and permanently blocked writer. Bride recalls telling Booker that her mother hated her black skin. She remembers Booker saying, "Scientifically there's no such thing as race."

Booker recalls the day he first saw Bride. "[D]umbstruck by her beauty," he decided to play his trumpet alone in the rain:

Still in thrall to the sheer beauty of the girl he had seen, he put the trumpet to his lips. What emerged was music he had never played before. Low muted notes held long, too long, as the strains floated through drops of rain.

Booker and Bride finally get it together—and Bride becomes pregnant...

A child. New life. Immune to Evil or Illness, protected from kidnap, beatings, rape, racism, insult, hurt, self-loathing, abandonment. Error-free. All goodness. Minus wrath.
So they believe.

In the book's final chapter, Sweetness, now 63 and in a nursing home, takes stock:

The last time I saw her she looked so good, I forgot about her color.... Now she's pregnant.
Listen to me. You are about to find out what it takes, how the world is, how it works and how it changes when you are a parent.
Good luck and God help the child.

P.S. Am I the only person who wonders why TM slightly altered the title of Billie Holiday's song "God Bless the Child"? Does it make you think of Billie's other masterpiece, "Strange Fruit," and flash back to *Beloved*? Is this another way Morrison's books say hello to each other?

APPENDIX: WORKS BY TONI MORRISON

Novels

The Bluest Eye. New York: Holy, Rinehart and Winston, 1970

Sula. New York: Alfred A. Knopf, 1973

Song of Solomon. New York: Alfred A. Knopf, 1977

Tar Baby. New York: Alfred A. Knopf, 1981

Beloved. New York: Alfred A. Knopf, 1987

Jazz. New York: Alfred A. Knopf, 1992

Paradise. New York: Alfred A. Knopf, 1997

Love. New York: Alfred A. Knopf, 2003

A Mercy. New York: Alfred A. Knopf, 2008

Home. New York: Alfred A. Knopf, 2012

God Help the Child. New York: Alfred A. Knopf, 2015

Short Fiction

"Recitatif" (1983)

Plays and Librettos

Dreaming Emmett (stage drama, debut 1986)

Margaret Garner (opera, debut 2005)

Desdemona (opera, debut 2011)

Nonfiction

The Black Book (1974)

Unspeakable Things Unspoken: The Afro-American Presence in American Literature, 1988

Playing in the Dark: Whiteness and the Literary Imagination, 1992

Race-ing Justice, En-gendering Power: Essays on Anita Hill, Clarence Thomas, and the Construction of Social Reality, ed., 1992

Birth of a Nation'hood: Gaze, Script, and Spectacle in the O.J. Simpson Case, co-ed., 1997

Remember: The Journey to School Integration, 2004

What Moves at the Margin: Selected Nonfiction, edited by Carolyn C. Denard, 2008

Burn This Book: Essay Anthology, ed., 2009

BIBLIOGRAPHY AND FURTHER READING

Anderson, S.E. *The Black Holocaust for Beginners*. Danbury, CT: For Beginners, 1995.

Bakerman, Jane. "The Seams Can't Show: An Interview with Toni Morrison." *Black American Literature Forum* 12:2, Summer 1978.

Beaulieu, Elizabeth Ann, ed. *The Toni Morrison Encyclopedia*: Westport, CT: Greenwood Press, 2003.

Bloom, Harold, ed. *Toni Morrison* (Bloom's Modern Critical Views). New York: Chelsea House, 2005.

Denard, Carolyn C., ed. *Toni Morrison: Conversations*. Jackson: University Press of Mississippi, 2008.

Gates, Henry Louis, Jr., and Appiah, Kwame A., eds. *Toni Morrison: Critical Perspectives, Past and Present*. New York: Amistad, 1993.

Kubitschek, Missy Dehn. *Toni Morrison: A Critical Companion*. Westport, CT: Greenwood Press, 1998.

McKay, Nellie Y., ed., *Critical Essays on Toni Morrison*. Boston, MA: G.K. Hall, 1988.

Seward, Adrienne Lanier, and Tally, Justine, eds., *Toni Morrison: Memory and Meaning*. Jackson: University Press of Mississippi, 2014.

Smith, Valerie, *Toni Morrison: Writing the Moral Imagination*. Malden, MA: Wiley, 2012.

Tally, Justine, ed. *The Cambridge Companion to Toni Morrison*. New York: Cambridge University Press, 2007.

Tate, Claudia. Interview with Toni Morrison. In *Black Women Writers at Work*, edited by Claudia Tate. New York: Continuum, 1983.

Taylor-Guthrie, Danielle, ed. *Conversations with Toni Morrison*. Jackson: University Press of Mississippi, 1994.

ABOUT THE AUTHOR

Ron David, a former editor-in-chief of the For Beginners series, is also the author of *Toni Morrison Explained: A Reader's Road Map to the Novels* (Random House, 2000). Previous works for For Beginners include *Arabs & Israel For Beginners, Jazz For Beginners* and *Opera For Beginners*. Ron has been a guest lecturer on all of these subjects across the United States, and he has been awarded a NJ State Council for the Arts fellowship for his novel-in-progress, *The Lebanese Book of the Dead*. He lives in Kihei, Hawaii, with his wife, the designer Susan David.

ABOUT THE ILLUSTRATOR

Dirk Shearer is a versatile freelance illustrator out of Pennsylvania. He's created editorial work for *Popular Science* magazine, logos for Ames True Temper, book illustrations for Boom! Studios, cover work for Archie Comics, a short comic for *Mouse Guard*, and product art for Spencer's Gifts, among many more. His pastimes include recreational sports, hiking, and riding his motorcycle.

THE FOR BEGINNERS® SERIES

ABSTRACT EXPRESSIONISM FOR BEGINNERS:	ISBN 978-1-939994-62-2
AFRICAN HISTORY FOR BEGINNERS:	ISBN 978-1-934389-18-8
ANARCHISM FOR BEGINNERS:	ISBN 978-1-934389-32-4
ARABS & ISRAEL FOR BEGINNERS:	ISBN 978-1-934389-16-4
ART THEORY FOR BEGINNERS:	ISBN 978-1-934389-47-8
ASTRONOMYFOR BEGINNERS:	ISBN 978-1-934389-25-6
AYN RAND FOR BEGINNERS:	ISBN 978-1-934389-37-9
BARACK OBAMA FOR BEGINNERS, AN ESSENTIAL GUIDE:	ISBN 978-1-934389-44-7
BEN FRANKLIN FOR BEGINNERS:	ISBN 978-1-934389-48-5
BLACK HISTORY FOR BEGINNERS:	ISBN 978-1-934389-19-5
THE BLACK HOLOCAUST FOR BEGINNERS:	ISBN 978-1-934389-03-4
BLACK PANTHERS FOR BEGINNERS:	ISBN 978-1-939994-39-4
BLACK WOMEN FOR BEGINNERS:	ISBN 978-1-934389-20-1
BUDDHA FOR BEGINNERS	ISBN 978-1-939994-33-2
BUKOWSKI FOR BEGINNERS	ISBN 978-1-939994-37-0
CHICANO MOVEMENT FOR BEGINNERS	ISBN 978-1-939994-64-6
CHOMSKY FOR BEGINNERS:	ISBN 978-1-934389-17-1
CIVIL RIGHTS FOR BEGINNERS:	ISBN 978-1-934389-89-8
CLIMATE CHANGE FOR BEGINNERS:	ISBN 978-1-939994-43-1
DADA & SURREALISM FOR BEGINNERS:	ISBN 978-1-934389-00-3
DANTE FOR BEGINNERS:	ISBN 978-1-934389-67-6
DECONSTRUCTION FOR BEGINNERS:	ISBN 978-1-934389-26-3
DEMOCRACY FOR BEGINNERS:	ISBN 978-1-934389-36-2
DERRIDA FOR BEGINNERS:	ISBN 978-1-934389-11-9
EASTERN PHILOSOPHY FOR BEGINNERS:	ISBN 978-1-934389-07-2
EXISTENTIALISM FOR BEGINNERS:	ISBN 978-1-934389-21-8
FANON FOR BEGINNERS:	ISBN 978-1-934389-87-4
FDR AND THE NEW DEAL FOR BEGINNERS:	ISBN 978-1-934389-50-8
FOUCAULT FOR BEGINNERS:	ISBN 978-1-934389-12-6
FRENCH REVOLUTIONS FOR BEGINNERS:	ISBN 978-1-934389-91-1
GENDER & SEXUALITY FOR BEGINNERS:	ISBN 978-1-934389-69-0
GREEK MYTHOLOGY FOR BEGINNERS:	ISBN 978-1-934389-83-6
HEIDEGGER FOR BEGINNERS:	ISBN 978-1-934389-13-3
THE HISTORY OF CLASSICAL MUSIC FOR BEGINNERS:	ISBN 978-1-939994-26-4
THE HISTORY OF OPERA FOR BEGINNERS:	ISBN 978-1-934389-79-9
ISLAM FOR BEGINNERS:	ISBN 978-1-934389-01-0
JANE AUSTEN FOR BEGINNERS:	ISBN 978-1-934389-61-4
JUNG FOR BEGINNERS:	ISBN 978-1-934389-76-8
KIERKEGAARD FOR BEGINNERS:	ISBN 978-1-934389-14-0
LACAN FOR BEGINNERS:	ISBN 978-1-934389-39-3
LIBERTARIANISM FOR BEGINNERS:	ISBN 978-1-939994-66-0
LINCOLN FOR BEGINNERS:	ISBN 978-1-934389-85-0
LINGUISTICS FOR BEGINNERS:	ISBN 978-1-934389-28-7
MALCOLM X FOR BEGINNERS:	ISBN 978-1-934389-04-1
MARX'S DAS KAPITALFOR BEGINNERS:	ISBN 978-1-934389-59-1
MCLUHAN FOR BEGINNERS:	ISBN 978-1-934389-75-1
MORMONISM FOR BEGINNERS	ISBN 978-1-939994-52-3
MUSIC THEORY FOR BEGINNERS:	ISBN 978-1-939994-46-2
NIETZSCHE FOR BEGINNERS:	ISBN 978-1-934389-05-8
PAUL ROBESON FOR BEGINNERS:	ISBN 978-1-934389-81-2
PHILOSOPHY FOR BEGINNERS:	ISBN 978-1-934389-02-7
PLATO FOR BEGINNERS:	ISBN 978-1-934389-08-9
POETRY FOR BEGINNERS:	ISBN 978-1-934389-46-1
POSTMODERNISM FOR BEGINNERS:	ISBN 978-1-934389-09-6
PRISON INDUSTRIAL COMPLEX FOR BEGINNERS:	ISBN 978-1-939994-31-8
PROUST FOR BEGINNERS:	ISBN 978-1-939994-44-8
RELATIVITY & QUANTUM PHYSICS FOR BEGINNERS:	ISBN 978-1-934389-42-3
SARTRE FOR BEGINNERS:	ISBN 978-1-934389-15-7
SAUSSURE FOR BEGINNERS:	ISBN 978-1-939994-41-7
SHAKESPEARE FOR BEGINNERS:	ISBN 978-1-934389-29-4
STANISLAVSKI FOR BEGINNERS:	ISBN 978-1-939994-35-6
STRUCTURALISM & POSTSTRUCTURALISM FOR BEGINNERS:	ISBN 978-1-934389-10-2
WOMEN'S HISTORYFOR BEGINNERS:	ISBN 978-1-934389-60-7
UNIONS FOR BEGINNERS:	ISBN 978-1-934389-77-5
U.S. CONSTITUTIONFOR BEGINNERS:	ISBN 978-1-934389-62-1
ZEN FOR BEGINNERS:	ISBN 978-1-934389-06-5
ZINN FOR BEGINNERS:	ISBN 978-1-934389-40-9

www.forbeginnersbooks.com